Death by C

by Paul Freed

Baker's Plays
c/o Samuel French, Inc.
45 West 25 Street
New York, NY 10010
bakersplays.com

NOTICE

FOR JACK WELCH
Because of him.

PROLOGUE
One tragic moment on a tragic night

ACT ONE

Scene One
Several weeks later. Morning

Scene Two
Afternoon

ACT TWO

Scene One
Evening

Scene Two
Night

Scene Three
Much later that night

EPILOGUE
The next day. Mid-afternoon

CAST OF CHARACTERS

Lady Riverdale — *Owner of Lady Riverdale Chocolates, Inc. and the new owner of the Meadowbrook Health Resort. She is the pompous, high-society type except when occasionally required to use a "vicious street shrewdness" to survive (which serves as a hint of her mysterious past).*

Dyslexia — *Lady Riverdale's assistant and long-suffering secretary on loan to...*

John Stone — *The new manager of the Meadowbrook Health Resort (and how he got there, no one knows). He is quick-witted and finds almost everything absurd (a basic cynical sort of person).*

Ralph Deadwood — *The Gym Manager and all-round cad. Knowing all about Lady Riverdale's past, he has used that knowledge to get whatever he can from her.*

Margaret Daniels — *A very attractive woman who is trying to write a feature story on the resort for a leading gossip magazine.*

Alfred Mellox — *He is in charge of the janitorial staff and maintenance for the resort (a position given to him only because he was the trusted companion of the late Henry Meadowbrook). He is very stiff, rigid, and typical "butler-type" with clipped British accent.*

Edith Chiles — *The Head Chef (or would that be, "Cheftess"?). She is a rather large, buxom sort of woman with jovial personality and New England Matronly manners (whatever that means).*

"Sweet Pea" Meadowbrook — *Daughter of the late Henry Meadowbrook. Extremely overweight, she seems to be trying to eat*

CAST OF CHARACTERS
(continued)

herself to death because of the trauma of losing her father. Her mouth is always full of food and no one can understand her without the help of Alfred Mellox.

Dick Simmering — *The Aerobics Instructor. Always garbed in a jogging outfit, he is a bright, hyperactive, effeminate person.*

Anne — *The resort nurse who tends to panic at the slightest injury.*

Ed Parlor — *Guest of Lady Riverdale's, he is a writer with a cheery disposition and enjoys the opportunity to try and solve the mysterious deaths by chocolate.*

Henry Meadowbrook — *The founder of the Meadowbrook Health Resort, he is never seen since he dies in the opening moments of the play.*

SETTING

The Meadowbrook Health Resort, a converted mansion in Upstate New York. All scenes take place in the Main Office which is a converted drawing room inside the converted mansion.

TIME

The Eve of the Grand Re-Opening of the Meadowbrook Health Resort after several weeks of dormancy following the death of Henry Meadowbrook.

DEATH BY CHOCOLATE

PROLOGUE

As CURTAIN opens we see a dimly-lit office — lit only by the light of night coming through the window and a small desk lamp which gives only a faint outline of HENRY MEADOWBROOK working studiously. The bookcase slowly opens and a hand holding a revolver stretches to Meadowbrook's head and fires. It withdraws as MEADOWBROOK slumps over, knocking the lamp off the desk and putting it out. With only the light through the windows we see ALFRED MELLOX come through the door — pauses — surveys the scene. He mutters: Oh look at this mess! *He rushes around the desk to the bookcase — disappears behind it for only a second or two. While it is still difficult to see, we can make out that he returns from the bookcase and puts something (a gun) in the hands of MEADOWBROOK. He closes the bookcase, fixes his hair, adjusts the various set pieces — furniture / hand props, collects his wits and begins to shout in panic:* HELP, HELP! Mr. Meadowbrook has killed himself!! *He rushes offstage screaming in panic. His voice echoing as the lights fade to BLACKOUT.*

7

ACT ONE
Scene One

Several weeks later. It is morning on the eve of the Grand Re-Opening of the Meadowbrook Health Resort. Lights up on the Main (or Manager's) Office of the Resort. And just as the Resort itself is a converted mansion from some by-gone Victorian era, so the Office has the air of once being a drawing room or study. It is rather luxurious by most standards. An ornate oak door leading to the rest of the Resort can be seen Stage Left. As the eye travels from there towards Stage Right we can see a quaint fireplace, wood paneling, a wall-sized bookshelf covered with old books, various paintings (including one of Henry Meadowbrook himself), and two French-style doors leading off to a patio Stage Right. By way of furniture, there is a large desk in front of the bookshelf and placed appropriately to that, several plush chairs, a couch (in front of the fireplace but facing the audience since it is warm weather), and any other endtables and ornaments which might add to the atmosphere of the room and the play itself. LADY RIVERDALE enters through the doors Stage Left followed by DYSLEXIA.

LADY R. That was quite a storm we had last night, eh, Dyslexia? I hardly slept a wink.

DYSLEXIA. Yes, ma'am. I had the same problem. The state police say that the bridge was flooded out.

LADY R. Not for long, I hope.

DYSLEXIA. No, they'll have it in operating order sometime today.

LADY R. Good. I don't want anything to interfere with our Grand Re-Opening tomorrow. Even if I have to get someone to lay down across the road.

DYSLEXIA. *(Pulling a notepad from her pocket and making a note)* Yes, ma'am. It'll be a very important day for all of us.

LADY R. The social event of the season. We've worked very hard for this day. *(Notices a box of chocolates on the desk)* Oh, look. Somebody gave Mr. Stone a box of my chocolates. How nice. I suppose I should have done it myself to welcome him aboard. Where *is* Mr. Stone anyway? Is he awake?

DYSLEXIA. Yes, ma'am. I saw him jogging around the lobby this morning.

LADY R. He jogs? How impressive. *(Pauses, puzzled)* Around the lobby?

DYSLEXIA. Yes. He does a lap around the lobby and then has breakfast.

LADY R. Why doesn't he jog outside?

DYSLEXIA. He says it's too far.

LADY R. I see. *(Chuckles)* He is a rather unusual man, isn't he?

DYSLEXIA. Without speaking out of turn ... yes, he is, ma'am.

LADY R. Has he met with the staff yet?

DYSLEXIA. Not that I know of. I'm not sure that he's done anything at all yet.

LADY R. I'm sure he will. He's only been manager for a week. We must give him the benefit of the doubt. They say he's one of the best Resort managers around.

DYSLEXIA. *(Offhandedly)* I wonder who *they* are?

LADY R. *They. Them.* The people who know. I wanted to be very careful with who I chose to be manager. Why, Dyslexia? Are you concerned about something?

DYSLEXIA. No, ma'am. I suppose not.

LADY R. Out with it, young lady. What's on your mind?

DYSLEXIA. Nothing, really. It's just that he doesn't *seem* like the manager of a health resort. He seems more like the type of person who should be running a pool hall.

LADY R. Well, looks can be very deceiving. I'm sure that none of us are who we appear to be on the outside. Watch and see.

DYSLEXIA. Yes, ma'am. I'm sure you're right. First impressions can be very misleading.

LADY R. Absolutely. Under Henry Meadowbrook, this place almost went bankrupt. Now that *I* own it, I want it to be profitable. I believe that Mr. John Stone is the man to make it that way. I didn't build an empire in chocolate candy by surrounding myself with a bunch of dodos.

DYSLEXIA. Yes, ma'am. Will that be all?

LADY R. Yes. *(DYSLEXIA moves to exit, LADY R speaks hesitantly)* Dyslexia ...

DYSLEXIA. *(Turning to her)* Yes, ma'am?

LADY R. You're closer to the staff than I am. Is everyone ... happy?

DYSLEXIA. I wouldn't know. I suppose so.

LADY R. Alfred Mellox ... is he behaving normally? He was very dedicated to Mr. Meadowbrook, you know, and I'm sure that he hates me.

DYSLEXIA. I couldn't say one way or another. I've

known him only as long as you have. He certainly doesn't confide in me.

LADY R. No ... I don't suppose he would. Thank you, Dyslexia.

DYSLEXIA. Yes, ma'am. *(She moves to exit as JOHN STONE enters Stage Left)*

STONE. Good morning, Diptheria.

DYSLEXIA. Dyslexia. *(She exits)*

STONE. Geseuntheit. *(Moves to the French doors and throws them open)* What a beautiful morning! *(He breathes deeply, begins coughing)* I need a cigarette.

LADY R. *(Wags a finger at him)* Ah ah ah. This is a *health* resort. No smoking here, Mr. Stone.

STONE. Of course not, Lady Riverdale. I was just joking. I haven't had a cigarette in— oh— four or five days at least. I don't need them. I've quit plenty of times.

LADY R. Good. You certainly look refreshed. The storm didn't keep you up?

STONE. Storm?

LADY R. Yes. Didn't you hear all the noise?

STONE. I thought that was you snoring. The walls around here are awfully thin.

LADY R. It knocked the bridge out.

STONE. If you'd keep it in a glass on the nightstand you wouldn't have that problem. Did you find it?

LADY R. Find what?

STONE. Your bridge. Smile for me. *(Confused, she does)* Wonderful. *(Frowns)* Did you have spinach for breakfast?

LADY R. *(She puts her hand to her mouth)* Oh, my ...

STONE. Well, Lady Riverdale, I've been here only a

week and I feel like things are shaping up nicely.

LADY R. Really?

STONE. Yes. I've lost five pounds. I certainly couldn't gain weight with what they feed me here. How many variations of yogurt and cottage cheese can there be? Haven't they ever heard of *real* food like chocolate cake, burritos, or mashed potatoes and gravy? I must talk to the chef.

LADY R. Be gentle. Edith Chiles doesn't take well to criticism.

STONE. Edith Chiles?

LADY R. The chef.

STONE. You mean *the* Edith Chiles? The famous TV cook show hostess and writer? I used to watch her every day on channel 7. At least until they started showing "Gilligan's Island" on channel 4. I didn't realize she was our head cooker.

LADY R. Which brings me to my point.

STONE. I didn't know you had one.

LADY R. I think you should have a staff meeting to formally introduce yourself to everyone. Especially since we're Re-Opening tomorrow. They need to be aware of your presence.

STONE. But I didn't bring any.

LADY R. This is a critical time for the Meadowbrook Health Resort. Its chances of success are directly related to what happens tomorrow and what *you* do here. I have the utmost confidence in you. *(Moves to exit)*

STONE. That could be your first mistake.

LADY R. And please make yourself more visible in the halls. Some of the Board of Directors are here. *(Waves)*

Keep me posted. *(She exits left)*

STONE. I don't think you'll fit on the bulletin board. *(Moves to desk, looks at box of chocolates)* Awww ... a box of Lady Riverdale chocolates. How sweet. *(Tosses them back down)* Too sweet. *(Looks at intercom box)* I hate those things. *(Pushes button)* Dysentery. I need you.

MALE VOICE. *(Coming through the intercom)* Yeah and I need gastritis. This is the gym, fella.

STONE. Oh. *(Pushes another button)* Hey, Dysrrhythmias!

FEMALE VOICE. You're sick! *(DYSLEXIA enters un-noticed through door left)*

STONE. *(Pushing another button)* Hello ... Distemper?

DYSLEXIA. Dyslexia.

STONE. *(Still talking to box)* Yeah, you. Come in here, please. *(Glances up and sees her standing there, talks to box)* Never mind, you're already here.

DYSLEXIA. You needed something, sir?

STONE. Sir! My friends call me John. You can call me Mr. Stone.

DYSLEXIA. Yes, sir.

STONE. Take some shorthand.

DYSLEXIA. *(Takes pad from pocket and poises to write)* Yes, sir.

STONE. Better make it longhand. I don't know how to read shorthand.

DYSLEXIA. How about if I take it in shorthand and type it long hand?

STONE. Nah, this is going to Edith Chiles. You better make it long winded. *(Dictates)* Memo to Edith Chiles. Last night's supper was the worst liver I have ever had.

DYSLEXIA. *(Mumbling as she writes)* Liver ... worst.

STONE. Not liverwurst. Just the liver.

DYSLEXIA. Oh. *(Scratches it off)* Then what about the liverwurst?

STONE. We didn't have liverwurst.

DYSLEXIA. Yes, we did.

STONE. We did? Well, no wonder it tasted funny. Never mind, then, just tell her I want to see her.

DYSLEXIA. Anything else?

STONE. Yes. Ask Alfred if he can't get these blood stains out of this desk.

DYSLEXIA. He tried, sir.

STONE. Ask him to try again. They're very distracting. It's like trying to work on a Rorschach test.

DYSLEXIA. Yes, sir. It may be difficult for him, though. He's the one who found Mr. Meadowbrook the night he ... he ... *(Can't say it)*

STONE. So I've heard. But if he's going to be affected by memories of Mr. Meadowbrook everytime he turns around then he shouldn't have stayed on here. But don't worry. I'll handle it with tact and diplomacy.

DYSLEXIA. Will that be all?

STONE. Gather everyone up for a staff meeting. And find out who used the hot tub last. They left a ring and got the soap all squishy.

DYSLEXIA. Yes, sir. *(Moves to exit, he continues as she exits left)*

STONE. I'm missing my boat, too. I think someone stole it. Check everyone's luggage before they leave. *(To himself)* From now on I play in the jacuzzi. *(ALFRED enters left)*

ALFRED. You wanted me, Mr. Snyde?

STONE. Stone. Yeah. Now don't cry or traumatize yourself but I'd like you to try harder to get those blood stains out of my desk.

ALFRED. Yes, sir. But I'm going to have to take the desk out.

STONE. Take it out? But you just met.

ALFRED. To refinish it. That's the only way to get rid of the stains.

STONE. But what will I sleep on during business hours?

ALFRED. The couch is comfortable.

STONE. Too obvious. *(Sighs)* Let me think about it. I can't live without my desk.

ALFRED. Neither could Mr. Meadowbrook.

STONE. Obviously he couldn't live *with* it, either.

ALFRED. It wasn't the desk that killed him, sir.

STONE. I'm sure it wasn't, Alfred. But that's his business, not mine. We all make choices, Alfred, and we have to stick by them. Unfortunately, suicide requires more of a commitment than most. *(MARGARET DANIELS enters left)*

MARGARET. Knock, knock.

STONE. *(To Alfred)* And fix my door. It sounds like a woman's voice when people knock on it.

ALFRED. Yes, sir. *(He exits and MARGARET comes fully into the room)*

MARGARET. You must be John Stone.

STONE. Amazing how some people can guess a name right off the top of their heads. *(Puts hands behind his back)* Now can you tell me how many hands I'm holding behind my back?

MARGARET. I'm Margaret Daniels.

STONE. Wrong. Two. *(He holds them out)* See?

MARGARET. I'm with *Elite* magazine.

STONE. *Elite* magazine? Well, well, well ... I was just reading one of your articles this morning in the bathroom. It was the one about the paraplegic gymnast. I never realized how much one can do with a wheelchair these days. Could he really do a cartwheel?

MARGARET. I saw it with my own eyes.

STONE. Better yours than someone else's. How nice of you to stop by.

MARGARET. I've been here for two days. You've been avoiding me, Mr. Stone.

STONE. *(Innocently)* Moi?

MARGARET. Yes, you. I've been in this business long enough to know when I'm being avoided.

STONE. I'm just very shy of reporters. My intense dislike of them might have something to do with it.

MARGARET. People who don't like reporters usually have something to hide. Could you be hiding something?

STONE. If I were, *you* wouldn't guess it. You couldn't even tell me how many hands I had behind my back.

MARGARET. With or without your cooperation, I'm going to write a feature on the Re-Opening of this place. Your cooperation will certainly help you. Let's face it, a favorable article in our magazine could do wonders for your business. I'm sure it hasn't been booming since Henry Meadowbrook's suicide.

STONE. It wasn't booming *before* his suicide either.

That's why we closed down to redo everything.

MARGARET. If nothing else, the article will be timely. Health is very popular these days.

STONE. Yeah, but you know how trends are. Yesterday it was the Hula Hoop, today physical fitness. A year from now garages will be filled with unused designer sweat suits, diet plans, and aerobics instructors.

MARGARET. Can I quote you on that? *(She takes out pad and pen)*

STONE. Quote me on anything you like. I'm sure you will whether I've said it or not.

MARGARET. Let me ask you a couple of questions then. Just to get my facts straight.

STONE. Facts! I thought you were writing for *Elite* magazine— exposer of the rich, manipulator of the poor and for only $1.00 at your local grocery counter.

MARGARET. The Meadowbrook Health Resort was founded by Henry Meadowbrook in 1949. And he alone owned it up until several weeks ago when he ...

STONE. *(Sits down with feigned pain)* Don't say it.

MARGARET. Oh. You and Henry Meadowbrook were close? I didn't think you knew one another.

STONE. Let me just say that when I sit down at this desk, I see him all over it.

MARGARET. How touching.

STONE. It was a tragedy.

MARGARET. *(Continuing)* Before he — well, you know — he was bought out by Lady Riverdale. Some say that he was *forced* to sell out.

STONE. *(Leaping to his feet)* That's outrageous! Who would say such a thing?

MARGARET. Almost everyone.

STONE. *(Suddenly calm)* Oh. Well, I'm not at liberty to discuss details but ... Henry Meadowbrook had problems of his own.

MARGARET. Oh?

STONE. Gambling debts, excessive drinking, crooked teeth, fallen arches, excessive nostril hair ...

MARGARET. Isn't a health resort a rather strange purchase for Lady Riverdale? She's known the world over for her *chocolate* company.

STONE. I can't speak for Lady Riverdale. In fact, I can't even do a good impersonation.

MARGARET. Yes, but chocolate and a health resort? It seems rather contradictory.

STONE. Life is full of contradictions, my dear. You can quote me on that.

MARGARET. No, thanks. I'm not looking for philosophical quotes, Mr. Stone. I want dirt.

STONE. Have you looked under your fingernails?

MARGARET. I want the untold story behind this health business. Whatever you can do will help. *(Stands)*

STONE. Would you like me to throw a physical fit?

MARGARET. I would like you to cooperate.

STONE. Cooperation is my middle name. My parents picked it at random from a thesaurus. Come to my room later tonight and I'll tell you how I got my last name.

MARGARET. I'll take a rain check. *(Moves to exit)*

STONE. Call the Weather Bureau. And while you're here you might want to consider our Thigh Thinner plan. *(She stops mid-stride to consider what he is implying, glances at her thighs and then exits left. RALPH DEADWOOD enters looking behind him—watching Margaret Stone walk away. He grunts, impressed)* I guess that just about says it all.

Knocking wouldn't be in your vocabulary, would it?

RALPH. I wouldn't knock *that*. Who is she?

STONE. A reporter. So keep your overactive glands on a leash. And while you're at it, leaving would be a nice idea.

RALPH. Aw, Mr. Stone, is that any way to talk to an old friend who you haven't seen in---oh, how long has it been?

STONE. Not long enough. The last time I saw you I got swindled out of $400 and almost went to jail. What are you doing here, Ralph? Did somebody throw you out of your gutter? No, forget it. I don't know what you're doing here. I don't want to know anything about you. Just leave. I'm sure you can't afford to be here anyway.

RALPH. That's always been your problem, John—you're too negative. And you're not too observant either. You've been here a week and you haven't noticed that I'm the Gym Manager. (*He sprawls out on the couch*)

STONE. The Gym Manager! Now I know who left the ring in the hot tub. You probably stole my boat, too. What do *you* know about managing a gym?

RALPH. As much as you know about managing a health resort.

STONE. In that case, you're fired.

RALPH. (*Laughs*) You can't fire me without Lady Riverdale's okay. And I know for a fact that she won't let you.

STONE. Oh, you and Lady Riverdale are pretty chummy, huh?

RALPH. You could say that I have somewhat of a hold on her.

STONE. Probably a half-nelson.

RALPH. She has great confidence in my abilities.

STONE. Yes, but what about managing the gym?

RALPH. My works speaks for itself.

STONE. So does your dishonesty.

RALPH. You don't like it? Let's see you do something about it.

STONE. That sounds like a dead, Darewood—a *dare,* Deadwood.

RALPH. Call it what you want, Stone. I'm here and there's nothing you can do about it.

STONE. We'll see about that. *(Pauses, notices how "at home" Ralph has made himself)* Are you comfy, Ralph? Can I get you anything? We're going to have a staff meeting now. It won't bother you will it?

RALPH. It never has before.

STONE. Good. Since you're such good friends with Lady Riverdale, I wouldn't want you to be upset. *(Moves to exit)* I'm going to find the rest of my staff now. Help yourself to anything I have. Especially the arsenic in the upper right hand drawer of the desk. *(Calls as he exits)* Exlaxia! *(Exits left. RALPH laughs to himself and props his feet up. LADY RIVERDALE enters—stops when she sees Ralph. Turns to exit left again)*

RALPH. *(Calling nonchalantly)* Lady Riverdale ...

LADY R. I will not remain alone in a room with you.

RALPH. *(Jumps up)* Not so fast. We have things to discuss. *(He moves left, peeks into the hall and closes door)*

LADY R. I have nothing to discuss with you.

RALPH. You have plenty, toots.

LADY R. Don't call me "toots."

RALPH. How about "Bubbles?"

LADY R. You're a pig, Ralph.

RALPH. Now, now, is that anyway to talk?

LADY R. There's a lot more I'd like to say.

RALPH. There's more *I* could say as well. But we wouldn't want me to do that, would we?

LADY R. *(Resigning herself)* No. I suppose not. What do you want from me now? And make it quick, you give me high blood pressure.

RALPH. I have a great idea. *(She doesn't respond, he looks at her)* You're supposed to say: "What's your great idea, Ralph?"

LADY R. *(Beginning to fan herself with her hand, speaks in a monotone)* What's your great idea, Ralph?

RALPH. I'm going to write a fitness book.

LADY R. You're going to .... I don't believe you.

RALPH. *(Begins posing, flexing muscles)* I'm going to write my own fitness book and maybe even pose for the pictures myself.

LADY R. Ha.

RALPH. I'd be a natural! A book, possibly a video program. I can't decide what to call it.

LADY R. "Become a Neanderthal in Ten Days."

RALPH. Don't mock me, Lady Riverdale. I'm very serious about this.

LADY R. Fine, Ralph. I wish you the best of luck.

RALPH. I don't want your wishes. You're going to help me finance it.

LADY R. Over my dead body.

RALPH. However you prefer.

LADY R. Or *your* dead body. You're out of your mind.

RALPH. Am I? Fitness books are the big sellers now. Everybody wants to know how to have bigger busts, thinner thighs, firmer fannies, slimmer stomachs .... we are obsessed with ourselves! What an easy way to make a fortune!

LADY R. Those books are written by models and movie stars and you are neither. In fact, you're hardly human.

RALPH. The way you flatter me. Then we'll do a fitness book for the average person. A book that the average jerk can use.

LADY R. You'd be ideal.

RALPH. You're in, then.

LADY R. No. I don't want anything to do with you or your scheme. I wish you were out of my life.

RALPH. I love you, too. But I don't think you have a choice about that.

LADY R. Maybe I do.

RALPH. *(Laughs)* Only if you kill me, my dear. Only if you kill me. *(She looks at him as if considering the idea when there is a knock at the door. STONE peeks in)*

STONE. Hi, kids. Am I interupting something? *(LADY R and RALPH speak together)*

LADY R. No.   RALPH. Yes.

STONE. *(Stepping in)* Good. Lady Riverdale, I was wondering if you could preoccupy our reporter friend so—

LADY R. Reporter friend?

STONE. From *Elite* magazine. She—

LADY R. She came! Wonderful. *(Moves to exit left)* Where is she? I'd love to talk with her.

STONE. You invited her?

LADY R. Of course! Publicity, Mr. Stone, publicity.

RALPH. We're not finished, *Lady* Riverdale.

LADY R. I think we are. *(She exits)*

STONE. *(To Ralph)* Yes, you certainly have a way with her.

RALPH. *(Angrily)* Maybe not now but I will. *(He plops down on the couch, folds his arms across his chest and broods. EDITH CHILES enters left)*

EDITH. Good morning, my children! How are we this morning?

RALPH. *(Rolls over away from them)* Oh, brother.

EDITH. *(Moving to Stone)* Mr. Stone, I presume.

STONE. *(Covers eyes, turns back to her)* Don't tell me. Let me guess .... Edith Chiles, world-famous television chef. *(Turns to face her)* I'd know you anywhere.

EDITH. How nice of you.

STONE. I read your cookbook, too. I was so impressed by the depth of your characters. And your writing style! So economical!

RALPH. *(Without turning)* So boring.

STONE. Is it true they're making it into a movie?

EDITH. I don't think so. Are you jesting with me, Mr. Stone? I'm not very good with subtle humor.

STONE. I assure you that I'm the least subtle person you'll ever meet.

RALPH. And the least humorous.

STONE. *(To Ralph)* Ralph, why don't you go find a pea shooter and do a lobotomy on yourself?

EDITH. Have you *really* seen my show, Mr. Stone?

STONE. Absolutely! In fact, when you walked in here I almost didn't recognize you without snow and static all over your picture. I'm so used to seeing you bending over a hot oven. To think that you're here now bending over on behalf of the Meadowbrook Health Resort. *(A beat)*

EDITH. Cancellation will do that. But enough of this flattery. I have a pheasant that needs preparation. Your assistant said that you wanted to see me.

STONE. I did?

EDITH. Something about last night's dinner?

STONE. Oh yeah! The liverwurst! By far the best I've ever had. My compliments.

EDITH. *(Laughs)* My dear, dear boy. That wasn't liverwurst.

STONE. It wasn't? Then I take it all back. It was terrible.

EDITH. It was Danish Liver Paté. A specialty from Minnesota.

STONE. You had it delivered all the way from there?

EDITH. *(Kisses fingers in appreciation)* It's a wonderful dish. I featured it on my show— number 237, I believe. It was very successful. We received many cards and letters about it.

STONE. Any threats?

EDITH. First you preheat your oven to 350 degrees then grind 1 pound of pork liver with 3/4 pound of pork fat along with—

STONE. Time out. Why don't you just make a video for me?

EDITH. Oh, yes, I *do* get carried away. But I love cooking so much. It's my life. I believe that everyone should do it. *You* should do it.

STONE. Hot dogs and frozen pizzas are my specialty.

EDITH. Tsk, tsk. There is little that compares to the joy of good, healthy eating. *(Sees chocolate on the desk)* Is that a box of Lady Riverdale chocolates?

STONE. Huh? *(She gestures to box on desk)* Yes. Would you like one?

EDITH. *(Giggles)* I really shouldn't but I've been having a taste for something sweet all morning. *(She takes a chocolate out of the box and bites into it)* Simply wonderful. Back to my kitchen!

STONE. Ms. Chiles, we're going to have a staff meeting now.

EDITH. Now? Oh, but I can't! I can hardly afford to be away from my kitchen *this* long with all I have to do for tomorrow. You must understand ...

STONE. Well .... okay ... but you're gonna miss a humdinger of a speech I've prepared. *(To Ralph)* No cracks from you.

EDITH. I will come back if I can.

STONE. Fine.

EDITH. *Bon apetite,* my children. *(She exits left)*

RALPH. *(An aside)* I don't think that woman's playing with a full deck.

STONE. She must be doing something right. She's made millions by smiling and cooking. She's like the mother that everyone remembers but no one had.

RALPH. *(Sits up)* *My* mother wasn't like that.

STONE. I'm not surprised.

RALPH. *(Stands)* And I think your staff meeting is a bust. I'm going back to the gym.

STONE. Relax. Everyone'll be here in a minute. *(Moves to exit left as ALFRED enters)* Alfred, where *is* everyone?

ALFRED. I don't know, sir. *(STONE groans and exits left. ALFRED goes to the fireplace and stands quietly. RALPH immediately begins provoking him)*

RALPH. How's it going, Al?

ALFRED. *(Looks at him with mild tolerance)* Alfred.

RALPH. Sure. Y'know, you look so at home in front of that fireplace. It's like you've always been there. Bet you two were built around the same time.

ALFRED. Are you trying to make some sort of point or is this your attempt at humor?

RALPH. Neither. I was just wondering how long you've been around here. You were Henry Meadowbrook's protege for a long time. 20 years was it? That's a long time to work for one man. It must have been a terrible shock to find him in here blown to pieces. They say you screamed, Al. Screamed like a *woman.* But then, that's what you really are, isn't it? You're certainly not a man. I understand that you spent 20 years being trampled underfoot by Henry Meadowbrook. Now, a real man wouldn't let that happen to him, would he? *(Pauses, eyes him closely, tauntingly)* Why are you still here, Al? Why didn't you just fade away after Meadowbrook killed himself? This is a different place now and you don't belong here.

ALFRED. I know more about health and exercise than you'll ever figure out.

RALPH. You know the old ways, Al, the *old* ways. Times

have changed. Now this is going to be a *real* health resort where we'll mold men into men and women into the deliciously curved women they should be.

ALFRED. *(Sarcastically)* Yes, this *is* the Enlightened Generation, isn't it?

RALPH. It's Rome, it's Greece, it's the new Sparta where only the fittest survive and the fat, weak and infirmed can die off. Sweat and agony, Al. "No pain, no gain" is the name of the game. Tightness of muscle and tautness of flesh. No more fat executives coming here to sit on their fat cigar butts pretending to get healthy. No, sir, fat is *very* out now and muscles are *in.* We're producing *real* men here. Now is the time for men to exemplify what it is to be real *men. (As a contrast to that bold declaration, DICK SIMMERING enters. As he speaks and finds a chair, both RALPH and ALFRED watch silently)*

DICK. *(Waving)* Good morning, boys! A beautiful day today, isn't it? *(He sits down primly, crossing his legs and placing his hands on his knees, smiling patiently)*

ALFRED. *(To Ralph)* You were saying?

RALPH. I didn't say the job was finished. *(To Dick)* Hi ho, Dick. Do you have your *aerobics* classes planned out for the big day tomorrow?

DICK. *(Excited)* Oh, yes! I'm very excited. *(Squirms, wiggles)* I can't wait to get going.

RALPH. Don't have an accident.

DICK. You should come in and join us sometime. It's very stimulating — the throbbing beat of the music, all those bodies moving and thrusting—

RALPH. —fat women in tights with rolls of flesh bouncing and jiggling as they grunt and snort with the smell of

Vaporub and Desenex—

DICK. *(Smiling at the thought)* Oh, yes ... pure heaven.

RALPH. It's sissy. You sweet sensitive guys drive me crazy. Aerobics is a wimp's way out of good hard exercise. You wanna get in shape? Pump some iron.

DICK. How vulgar. You get blisters and break nails ... it's disgusting.

RALPH. You're a wimp.

DICK. Sticks and stones may break my bones—

RALPH. They wouldn't if you'd lift weights. *(SWEET PEA MEADOWBROOK enters left. She moves to couch and sits down, munching on snacks the whole way)*

DICK. Hi, Sweet Pea. Are you going to be in my aerobics class?

RALPH. She's a class by herself.

DICK. Be nice.

RALPH. Hey, Sweet Pea, Amahl the Tentmaker called and said your new dress is ready. *(She looks hurt. ALFRED steps forward to her defense)*

ALFRED. Can you show just a little compassion? The poor girl's father committed suicide. It's bad enough that she has to come into this office at all. The memories must be heartbreaking. *(She mumbles in acknowledgement)* That's right, dear. Pay him no mind.

RALPH. Well, why does she have to eat all the time? For crying out loud, it's ... nauseating just to look at her.

ALFRED. She eats because she is traumatized over losing her father like she did. Her psychiatrist says she'll get better soon.

RALPH. If she doesn't explode first.

ALFRED. Imagine what it must be like — the only

daughter of Henry Meadowbrook, a young woman with a bright future, the world at her feet, social standing, good credit — and to have it suddenly snuffed out and be left virtually penniless. *(As he speaks, SWEET PEA nods in pitiful agreement)*

DICK. *(Choking up with tears)* Terrible.

ALFRED. Put yourself in her shoes.

RALPH. I could put both my feet in one of her shoes.

ALFRED. *(Patting her reassuringly)* But you'll get better, Sweet Pea. *(She shakes her head no)* You'll get over this and be the woman you once were.

RALPH. Instead of the *three* she is now. *(ANNE enters hurriedly — as if late)*

ANNE. Am I late? *(She finds a place to be comfortable)*

DICK. No.

ANNE. Oh, good. I was trying to get the infirmary ready for tomorrow. I've been sterilizing *everything*.

RALPH. I better stay away from the infirmary then.

DICK. You're sick. Is that all you ever think about?

RALPH. No, I like to eat and sleep, too.

ANNE. *(To Alfred)* What are they talking about? I don't understand.

ALFRED. Never mind, Anne. Never mind. *(LADY R, STONE and DYSLEXIA enter left and find appropriate places to stand for the meeting. LADY R and STONE should be near the desk as the center of attention)*

LADY R. It looks as if everyone is here. Except Edith, of course.

STONE. What did you do with Ms. Daniels, the reporter?

LADY R. She's taking a sauna.

STONE. I hope she doesn't take it too far. We'll need it for tomorrow.

LADY R. A sauna was the only way I could keep her away from this meeting.

STONE. I'll bet she's steamed.

LADY R. I think she should sit in on this meeting — to see how this resort does business.

STONE. I thought you wanted *good* publicity.

LADY R. *(Addresses everyone)* I'm not going to take too much of your time. I know you have many things left to do to make our Grand Re-Opening a huge success. But I felt that it's important for you to become acquainted with the man who will lead the Meadowbrook Health Resort to a glorious rebirth. *(STONE looks around for someone else)* A very talented, gifted man who will work the miracle we need to undo the chains of the past and—

STONE. Whadja do, hire someone behind my back?

LADY R. I'm talking about *you!*

STONE. Oh! *(Smiles smugly)* Then do go on.

LADY R. He is the one who will use his enormous creative resource to do whatever it takes to turn this resort around.

STONE. Short of resigning.

LADY R. He will guide us towards making the Meadowbrook Health Resort a respectable, credible—

STONE. —Profitable—

LADY R. —And profitable enterprise. He will banish the mistakes and ghosts of the past and bring new life to this hollow corpse. *(Getting carried away with her imagery as everyone shuffles impatiently)* Through the veins of this body we call a health resort, he will transfuse fresh blood, he will give mouth-to-mouth resuscitation to the very lips of this once-prestigious institution, he will massage the heart of—

STONE. *(Stepping forward)* All right, all right, take a breather from the anatomy lesson.

LADY R. Oh ... I'm sorry. This is John Stone. *(She steps away)*

STONE. Thank you, Lady Riverdale, for that poetic if not altogether disgusting introduction. My friends, as the new manager of the Meadowbrook Health Resort, I want to welcome you to a new era of fitness and good living. In this resort we hope to epitomize the self-worship that is so characteristic of our society today. Here we will celebrate the end of cellulite, we will become the foes of flabbiness, and win the war of weight control. We must put the past behind us and put our behinds in gear for the future. Together we will reach beyond fat farms of yesteryear to a new generation of physical excellence and meet it head-on with hope and the opportunity for every man, woman, and child to be men, women and children of this new era. We hold the key to the future in our hands — health! Where would people be without it? They would be *dead,* that's where! Well, at Meadowbrook Health Resort, nobody dies without trying to get healthy first. And that's our new motto, folks ... a motto that captures the essence of what we believe in: *Get Fit Or Die Trying!* *(Caught up in the passion of his speech, everyone applauds enthusistically)*

LADY R. Wonderful, wonderful! *(She steps forward)*

STONE. Hold it, I'm not done. *(Embarrassed, she steps*

back) Tomorrow is our big day, right?

EVERYONE. Right.

STONE. What sorts of special things do you have planned? *(They look at each other to see who will answer first. Finally...)*

DICK. I have a new batch of exercises worked up. *(Jumps up)* Do you want to see them?

EVERYONE. No.

STONE. Just tell us what they are.

DICK. Well, let's see ... there's the "Doggie Squat Bicycle Pump" and the "Thigh Thumping Trunk Turner" and the "Walking Through The Park Chest Expander" and—

STONE. Fine, fine, we understand.

RALPH. The "Doggie Squat Bicycle Pump?" That sounds ridiculous.

DICK. It's very hard. In fact, it's anatomically impossible. The women will love it. *(To Ralph)* Why? What do *you* have planned, Ralphie?

RALPH. A rigorous weight-lifting program. I'm going to explore dimensions of muscular pain they never knew existed.

DICK. Pain? Gee, I might try that myself.

STONE. Alfred, I want you to make sure that the rooms are in order. I want the odds on the left and the evens on the right. Tell the staff to leave them that way. I went down one hallway and they were turned around.

ALFRED. Yes, sir.

STONE. *(To Dyslexia)* Relaxia, I want the front desk covered at all times.

DYSLEXIA. But how will people sign the register?

STONE. You're right. Don't cover it. Just make sure someone's there all the time. *(Pause)* Well, I think that just about wraps it— *(Stops, notices Sweet Pea)* Who are you?

LADY R. That's Sweet Pea Meadowbrook. *(Whispers)* Daughter of Henry.

STONE. Oh. *(To Sweet Pea)* Hi, Sweet Pea. What are you going to do tomorrow?

(Mumbles something about eating all day)

STONE. *(Not comprehending, looks as if he did to avoid embarrassment)* Yes. I see. Good. Well, I think that just about wraps it up. I want to— *(He is interrupted by EDITH CHILES bursting into the room through the door left. She stumbles around, grabbing her throat and gasping for air)* Edith, glad you could join us. *(She wheezes and gasps)*

EDITH. *(Wheezing and gasping)* I ... I've ... *(EVERYONE realizes that she is in trouble and reacts accordingly)*

STONE. What's wrong? Too much seasoning on the pheasant?

EDITH. Poisoned! I've been... *(DICK jumps to her aid)*

DICK. She said she's been poisoned!

STONE. She's just being overly critical.

EDITH. Pheasant... do not... *(Her eyes roll up into their sockets as she twirls to collapse. DICK tries to catch her but discovers quickly that her weight is too much for him. With humorous awkwardness, he finds himself beneath her as they both slowly fall to the ground)*

DICK. *(Out of breath)* Help... *(This brings about total chaos as everyone tries to think of something — moving every which way)*

LADY R. Anne! You're the staff nurse! Do something!

(Panic) What should I do? I've only worked for spas. I only know how to take care of pulled groins and cramps and—

DICK. Help... *(STONE pulls on EDITH to try to get her up off of Dick but with no success)*

LADY R. Do something! *Anything!*

ANNE. All right... *(With that said, she faints)*

STONE. Hang on, Edith, we'll get an ambulance. *(He motions DYSLEXIA to the phone)*

DICK. I'm suffocating.

STONE. Edith ... can you hear me?

EDITH. Don't eat...

STONE. Don't eat?

EDITH. Don't eat choc—

STONE. Don't eat chalk. Okay, gotcha. What about erasers?

EDITH. Poison...

STONE. Yeah, I'll bet. Real killers. Blackboards, too.

EDITH. *(Overdramatically)* Bon apetite. *(She exhales deeply and goes to that Great Kitchen in the sky. The stage becomes deathly silent as everyone looks on)*

STONE. *(Checking her pulse)* She's gone to that great Gourmet Resort in the sky.

LADY R. *(Gasp)* You mean...

STONE. She's .... dead. *(They react with shock and pain)*

RALPH. There goes dinner. *(Blackout. Curtain)*

Scene Two

Later that afternoon. Curtain and lights up on stage. LADY RIVERDALE is pacing nervously. DYSLEXIA is finishing up a phone conversation at the desk. Note that Lady Riverdale's purse should be on the couch.

DYSLEXIA. Okay ... thank you. It was all just a misunderstanding. Right. *(She hangs up)*

LADY R. Well? Did they believe you?

DYSLEXIA. Yes, I suppose so. I told them that the call for an ambulance was a misunderstanding.

LADY R. I heard that part. What did *they* say?

DYSLEXIA. They said it was fine. There isn't much they can do anyway with the bridge still being repaired. It won't be ready until later today and they can't get up here until then.

LADY R. *(Sighs, relieved)* Good. Something like this could destroy our Grand Re-Opening tomorrow and I can't afford to let that happen.

DYSLEXIA. Anything else, ma'am?

LADY R. Yes. I want everyone who knows about this to understand that if they breathe a word of it to anyone that they'll be fired. Not only will they not work for me any-more — I'll see to it that they won't work for *anyone*. Ever. Understand? After all the money I've put into this resort, I won't have my Grand Re-Opening ruined by an accidental death.

DYSLEXIA. Accidental? But she said she was poisoned.

LADY R. *Accidental,* Dyslexia. You're dismissed.

DYSLEXIA. Yes, ma'am. *(She exits left. LADY R paces more furiously)*

LADY R. Oh, Edith, how could you do this to me? *"Bon apetite"* indeed! *(STONE enters left)*

STONE. We carried her to her room. *(Groans)* I think I have a double hernia.

LADY R. Did anyone see you?

STONE. No. All your Board Member friends took a dip in the pool.

LADY R. What about Margaret Daniels?

STONE. She's the dip they took in the pool.

LADY R. Thank heaven. I don't want anyone to know about this.

STONE. That'll be kinda hard once the ambulance arrives.

LADY R. The ambulance won't be coming.

STONE. What? *(Moves to desk)* I better call.

LADY R. No! Don't bother. We already did. They can't come because ... because the bridge is still being repaired.

STONE. What about a helicopter? They use helicopters on TV.

LADY R. They don't have one. Remember — we're out in the country here. *(She sits down, fans herself)* My blood pressure.

STONE. Then call for a buggy, a boat, a canoe! We can't leave Edith in her room.

LADY R. Why not? Nobody knows she's in there. She'll be fine. *(Pauses, changes to a more serious tone)* Mr. Stone, you realize the adversity that could be caused by Edith's death?

STONE. I know what it did to Edith.

LADY R. It could hurt our Grand Re-Opening.

STONE. It could. But, Lady Riverdale, Edith Chiles isn't just *dead* — she was poisoned.

LADY R. She died from her pheasant.

STONE. Then it was fowl play. *(A beat)* Sorry.

LADY R. We cannot let this affect our Grand Re-Opening, Mr. Stone.

STONE. Oh, so *that's* it! You're concerned about *money* ahead of a human life. How typical. How ... how utterly upper class!

LADY R. You have an investment in this as well.

STONE. *(Overdramatized disappointment)* Oh, Lady Riverdale. I'm so disappointed in you. Such a shameless display of greed. Where are your priorities? Your humanity? Your value of human life?

LADY R. You could get a substantial bonus.

STONE. A bribe? Are you trying to bribe me? *(Pause)* How much?

LADY R. Five percent.

STONE. Make it seven.

LADY R. Fine. Seven it is. *If* all goes smoothly with the Re-Opening tomorrow.

STONE. I must be nuts.

LADY R. Not nuts. Greedy.

STONE. The first sign of any trouble with this and it's all over. Understand? Whoever poisoned Edith Chiles is still on the loose.

LADY R. We don't know that she was poisoned.

STONE. *She* seemed to think so. And as the victim, I'm willing to take her word for it.

LADY R. Why would anyone want to poison Edith Chiles?

STONE. Maybe I wasn't the only one who didn't like her Danish Liver Paper Maché.

LADY R. Pate.

STONE. Pat-ty who?

LADY R. Not *who*. A dish.

STONE. She is? How do I meet her?

LADY R. Please, Mr. Stone, this isn't the time.

STONE. It would help if we could figure out her last words. What in the world did she mean by "Don't eat chalk?" *(He wanders to desk casually as he speaks)* Was it some sort of code? *(He also casually picks up box of chocolates and chooses one)* Maybe she was trying to say someone's name. *(He slowly lifts chocolate to take a bite)*

LADY R. There's no one here with a name like "chalk."

STONE. *(Lowers chocolate)* Yeah ... Chiles is the only thing that sounds even close. *(Lifts chocolate to bite again)*

LADY R. Maybe it was suicide.

STONE. *(Lowers chocolate)* Nah. She specifically said "chalk" — nothing else. Don't eat chalk. *(Lifts chocolate, stops)* Maybe "chalk" was short for something. *(Lifts chocolate to mouth when MARGARET DANIELS storms into the room angrily. Surprised, STONE puts the chocolate back in the box)*

MARGARET. Mister Stone! Lady Riverdale! Will *someone* please tell me what's going on? You promised to cooperate — both of you did — but I can't get a word out of anyone. No one is talking... about *anything!* I can't even get the time of day!

STONE. It's 1:45.

MARGARET. Something has happened. I can feel it in my gut.

STONE. That was lunch.

MARGARET. I want some information and I want it *now*.

STONE. *(Moving towards her to get her to the door)* Why don't you relax and take a sauna?

MARGARET. Sauna! I'm like a prune from being in the sauna so long.

STONE. Oh yeah? Lemme see.

MARGARET. Lady Riverdale ... *please*. It was your suggestion I come up here to begin with. I *do* want this article to be good. For your sake *and* mine.

LADY R. There's nothing really—

STONE. Okay, okay, you dragged it out of us.

MARGARET. What?

LADY R. What?!?

STONE. Since she wants to be such a nosey little nipper, I think we should spill it all.

LADY R. I don't know what you're saying. *(To Margaret)* He doesn't know what he's saying.

STONE. Of course I do. *(To Margaret)* We were going to have a surprise birthday party for you.

MARGARET. A surprise bir — but it's not my birthday!

STONE. Surprise!!

MARGARET. This is absurd. You don't want to cooperate? Fine. I'll kill you in print. My magazine has authorized me to do whatever it takes to get the inside story on this place. Even pay *money* for it. *(Moves left to exit)*

And what information I can't buy, I'll make up! *(She exits left)*

STONE. Ah ... a true journalist.

LADY R. *(Fanning herself furiously)* My blood pressure. I'm going to have a stroke. *(Stands)*

STONE. Take five, Lady R. Everything'll be fine. *(Speaks parenthetically)* He says to her in a soothing voice that refuses to betray his own deeper panic.

LADY R. I need some air. *(She moves right to patio doors and exits)*

STONE. *(Speaking after her)* No more than thirty-two pounds pressure. *(Begins thinking aloud to himself)* Don't eat chalk. Don't eat ... It's probably right under my nose. *(Sits down, puts face in hands)* Don't eat chalk. *(Unseen by Stone, DYSLEXIA slips in door left and moves to desk)*

DYSLEXIA. Sir?

STONE. *(Startled)* What?!?!

DYSLEXIA. I'm sorry.

STONE. Don't do that.

DYSLEXIA. There's a man outside who wishes to see you.

STONE. A man? What man?

DYSLEXIA. His name is Ed Parlor.

STONE. Ed Parlor?

DYSLEXIA. He's a guest of one of the board members. And a friend of Lady Riverdale's.

STONE. What does he want *me* for?

DYSLEXIA. He said he wants to talk to the manager. That's you.

STONE. Semantics. It's all a matter of semantics.

DYSLEXIA. Shall I send him in? *(ED PARLOR enters

casually left without being seen by either Stone or Dyslexia)

STONE. No. Take a message. I'm trying to solve a murder here.

PARLOR. A murder?

STONE. *(Surprised but hiding it)* Yes, this job is killing me.

DYSLEXIA. *(To Parlor)* Mr. Parlor, you shouldn't walk in like that.

PARLOR. I can't walk any other way. I'm chafing.

DYSLEXIA. Mr. Stone...

STONE. That's all right. *(Stands, waves her off)* I'll take it from here. Any friend of Lady Riverdale's is certainly a friend of Lady Riverdale's. *(DYSLEXIA — slightly annoyed — exits left. STONE remains standing)* What can I do for you, Mr. Powder? I hope your stay here has been enjoyable.

PARLOR. Parlor. Ed Parlor is my name. And my stay has been wonderful. I feel very priveleged getting to be here before your Grand Re-Opening. It's like a sneak preview.

STONE. Lady Riverdale wanted her investors to see their investment. Distemper, my secretary, said you're — what? A friend of the board, a member of the board, or are you just plain bored?

PARLOR. A friend. Actually, I'm a writer. I do novels, plays...

STONE. Anything dirty?

PARLOR. No.

STONE. Then I probably haven't read anything you've written.

PARLOR. I generally do murder-mysteries.

STONE. You've come to the right place.

PARLOR. Oh? Why is that?

STONE. The setting ... the country ... all of that. If we had a cliff we could be a gothic novel.

PARLOR. To be quite honest, Mr. Stone, I *am* here *because* of this setting. I'm writing a play — a murder-mystery. And the Meadowbrook Health Resort is ideal for it. It's called "Death By Chocolate."

STONE. You're kidding. Don't let Lady Riverdale hear that or she'll kill you.

PARLOR. Do you think she's capable?

STONE. It's just a figure of speech. I was referring to the fact that she owns a chocolate company. I don't think she'd be too happy with a play that implies that chocolate kills people. *(Begins chuckling)* It's a pretty ridiculous idea anyway.

PARLOR. I don't think so. I think it's perfect. Especially here — a dark gloomy mansion converted into a health resort ... the original owner commits suicide...

STONE. Boring. I'd never go see a play like that.

PARLOR. *(Lost in his thoughts)* Just imagine the opening! A dark stage — silent — until a shot rings out and somebody cries: *(Literally)* "Help! Help! Mr. Meadowbrook has killed himself!" *(This brings DYSLEXIA running through the door left and LADY RIVERDALE through the patio doors right)*

DYSLEXIA. Is everything all right?

LADY R. Good Lord, what's going on? *(PARLOR laughs)*

STONE. It'll never work.

PARLOR. I'm sorry. *(DYSLEXIA groans and exits left)*

LADY R. Ed! What in the world are you up to?

PARLOR. Just discussing my new play with Mr. Stone.

LADY R. Must you discuss it so *loudly?*

PARLOR. Why is everyone so jumpy?

LADY R. It's been a bad day. What does your screaming about Henry Meadowbrook have to do with a play?

PARLOR. That's the opening. But I won't use his name.

STONE. It's called "Death by Chocolate."

LADY R. Oh, Ed...

PARLOR. Nothing personal. The rest of the play will have little or no resemblance to this resort. I'll probably poison one or two of the characters — maybe the cook and somebody else inconsequential. See, I—

LADY R. The cook! *(Slumping into a chair)* I'm going to faint ... someone get some water...

STONE. That's the silliest plot I've ever heard of.

PARLOR. *(To Stone)* I don't understand. *(To Lady Riverdale)* Lady Riverdale?

LADY R. My Grand Re-Opening ... I can't bear it...

STONE. Let's leave her alone to be delirious for a few moments. This has been a stressful day. Let me show you the ivy we just put in on the side of the building. *(He guides PARLOR to patio doors right and they exit — PARLOR, perplexed and looking back to Lady R. LADY RIVERDALE tries to relax and collect her thoughts)*

LADY R. If I'd known big business was going to be this tough, I never would have left poverty. *(She pauses, thinks)* Death by Chocolate ... it sounds like a judgement. A curse. Maybe that's what this whole thing is ... a judge-ment on me. We sentence you to death by choc— *(She is interrupted by RALPH DEADWOOD'S appearance at the door. He saunters in)*

RALPH. *(Looking around)* Talking to yourself now?

LADY R. What do you want?

RALPH. Such hostility! *(Paces around her casually and moves to desk)* One day we *must* do something about that.

LADY R. Ralph, I'm really not in the mood for your remarks. It's been a terrible day.

RALPH. Awwww ... it's going to get worse, too. *(Picks up chocolate off of the desk and offers it to her)* Chocolate?

LADY R. No, thank you.

RALPH. *(He looks it over and pops it into his mouth)* I was just talking to that reporter lady from the gossip magazine.

LADY R. Margaret Daniels.

RALPH. Yeah. I think she has the hots for me.

LADY R. You think *every* woman has the hots for you.

RALPH. Did you know that her magazine pays big bucks for scandalous stories? I mean, *big* bucks. Not like the nickels and dimes *you* pay me.

LADY R. Nickels and dimes! *(Stands)* You blackmail me and have the nerve to call what I give you "nickels and dimes?"!! I shouldn't be giving you a cent!

RALPH. Yeah and you know what happens. But now the stakes are increased. Edith Chiles' untimely death sees to that. Imagine what it would do to your Grand Re-Opening if I told Margaret Daniels that Edith Chiles was poisoned and that you're trying to cover it up. Maybe you're also covering up the murderer's identity. Maybe *you* are the murderer!

LADY R. You've lost your mind.

RALPH. Have I? And what will the reaction by the public *and* your board of directors *and* your stockholders be when they discover that Lady Riverdale is a *fraud.* That Lady Riverdale was once Bubbles Malone — a strip tease artist! The pictures alone are worth a thousand words. Or thousands of dollars.

LADY R. *(Moves to her purse on the chair)* But I can't afford to give you anymore money.

RALPH. You're pretty resourceful when you want to be.

LADY R. *(Her voice softens, she sounds near tears)* But I'm not... This is all too much for me. *(She picks up her purse)* I need a tissue.

RALPH. Come on, Babs, don't give me those crocodile tears. My terms will be reasonable. What do you say?

LADY R. I hate you.

RALPH. Thanks. But that isn't the answer I'm looking for.

LADY R. You can forget about getting any more money from me.

RALPH. Tsk, tsk, tsk! *(Moves to door left)* I hate to see it end this way.

LADY R. *(Pulls revolver out of purse and points it at him)* Hold on, Ralph. I hate to see it end this way too. Put your hands up.

RALPH. *(Puts hands up)* Now, Babs, what do you think you're doing?

LADY R. Getting you out of my life after all these years.

RALPH. What good'll it do you? You pull that trigger and you'll be surrounded by four walls the rest of your life. A lot of good jail will do you.

LADY R. They won't send me to jail. It'll be a clear case of self-defense. In fact, Ralph, my love, you could be the answer to *all* my problems!

RALPH. I doubt it. The cops'll never believe self-defense.

LADY R. Sure they will when I tell them that it was you who poisoned Edith Chiles. I found out and when you knew that I knew you tried to kill *me*. We struggled... *(Pushes over the chair, tears the sleeve on her blouse)* ... and I shot you.

RALPH. You won't shoot me. You haven't got the nerve. *(He moves towards her. She extends the gun towards him, taking aim. He stops)*

LADY R. Don't be so sure, Ralph. You've haunted me for years — all the way from Bennie's Bar on 14th Street to where I am now. I've worked hard to make good — to be somebody — and you've trailed my every step. You've been nothing but a leech, Ralph. A monkey on my back. And I've reached the end of my rope. I'm putting the light back into my future by turning yours off. Goodbye, Ralph. *(She takes better aim and postures herself to shoot)*

RALPH. *(Begging)* No, Babs, don't do it. I won't tell. I'll leave! I promise!

LADY R. You think I'm stupid enough to believe that? *(She aims pistol, pulls trigger. The top pops up and reveals a flame. The pistol is a lighter)* Oops. I packed the wrong gun. *(RALPH begins to laugh. She throws the gun down furiously and he laughs harder)*

RALPH. You're such a foolish woman. *(He continues laughing until he suddenly begins to choke. Grabbing his throat, he stumbles and makes strangling noises. Overdramatically — and ridiculously — he moves around the room collapsing against the walls, the bookshelf — pulling books down — across the desk, into chairs, and finally onto the center stage floor — dead)*

LADY R. *(Surprised and suspicious)* Ralph? *(She checks his pulse, drops his hand with a lifeless thud and stands over the body)* Boy, that was easy. *(With that said, she screams as if in fright. STONE and PARLOR dash in through the patio doors right. STONE goes to Ralph to check him over while PARLOR takes hold of LADY RIVERDALE)*

STONE. Oh no ... not another.

PARLOR. Lady Riverdale, what has happened?

LADY R. Deadwood is ... dead!

STONE. Deadwood is dead?

LADY R. Dead. I think he was poisoned.

PARLOR. Poisoned!

LADY R. Just like Edith Chiles.

PARLOR. Edith Chiles!

STONE. Well, Parlor, you might just get a murder-mystery out of your stay here after all.

PARLOR. Poisoned? But how?

LADY R. *(Suddenly realizing)* Chocolate! He ate a piece of chocolate when he came in!

STONE. Of course! "Don't eat chalk" means "Don't eat chocolate!" That's what Edith was trying to say. They both had your chocolate and died from it. *(To Lady R)* I'm surprised you've been able to stay in business this long.

PARLOR. *(Pauses ominously)* I can't believe it. He died a ... death by chocolate. *(STONE and LADY RIVERDALE look at Parlor as the lights fade to blackout. Curtain)*

ACT TWO
Scene One

Evening. Stone's office. Everything is normal except that the book-case is pulled out like an open door. What's behind it cannot be seen by the audience. Quietly, looking to make sure no one is watching, PARLOR steps from behind the case and pushes it closed to it's original position. STONE enters. PARLOR tries to look non-chalant as he pulls a book from the shelf. STONE sees Parlor and steps back to look at the nameplate on the door.

STONE. Oh, this *is* my office. I thought I made a mistake.

PARLOR. I was just admiring your books.

STONE. *(Moves to desk)* They were Henry Meadow-brook's. I keep getting overdue notices from the library.

PARLOR. How was dinner?

STONE. Nobody died, if that's what you mean. But maybe that's because no one would eat. Except the Board of Directors. But, hey, what they don't know will probably kill them.

PARLOR. Then nobody but a handful of us know.

STONE. Lady Riverdale wants it to be our little secret until after the Grand Re-Opening. I'm tempted to call the police anyway. I get a little nervous when I think that someone is trying to kill me. Those chocolates *were* sent to me, you know.

PARLOR. Well, never fear, Stone. I've been doing a lot of thinking about this case. And some sneaking around.

STONE. So I could see. I don't know why I don't just put in a revolving door for this office.

PARLOR. This could work out better than any of us could have planned. I can put all of this in my play.

STONE. Edith and Ralph will be pleased to know that they gave up their lives for art. *(Pauses)* You know, I once read about a writer who had to act out his ideas before he could write them. You wouldn't be doing that with your play, would you? What's it called? "Death By Chocolate"?

PARLOR. *(Smiles)* Very good, Mr. Stone. Now you're beginning to think like a murder-mystery writer.

STONE. That doesn't flatter me. You guys give me the creeps the way you kill off people for the sake of a story. They're human beings.

PARLOR. They're characters of my imagination.

STONE. And *we're* characters of someone else's imagination and I don't like the idea of being killed. So there.

PARLOR. But that's the point! So far this is working out exactly as I would have written it. I was going to have only two deaths in my play. Both in the first act. None in the second act so we're safe.

STONE. Why none in the second act?

PARLOR. I don't want to overdo it for the audience. The second act involves sorting out the clues and finding the murderer. And the killer must be someone we know. It's always a character the audience has seen but might not suspect. We—the protagonists—assemble the clues and information and make an accusation.

STONE. Sounds wonderful.

PARLOR. But we'll be wrong.

STONE. Not so wonderful. Why will we be wrong?

PARLOR. To fool the audience and make us rethink our position. There has to be a wild goose chase or the play will end too quickly and the audience will feel like they didn't get their money's worth. And then—bingo!

STONE. We catch the killer.

PARLOR. No. We find a new piece of information that leads us in the right direction.

STONE. And what kind of information will we find, pray tell?

PARLOR. I'm not allowed to say until after we make an accusation. Just remember that no one is who they seem to be and everyone has secrets from the past.

STONE. But that's in a *play,* Parlor. This isn't a play! *(PARLOR and STONE pause, look at each other. A beat. They shrug)*

STONE. Okay, what do we do first?

PARLOR. *Everyone* is a suspect. Even you. Remember that.

STONE. Reminds me of my college days. How about you, are you a suspect?

PARLOR. Of course. You don't know that I'm *not* the kind of writer who acts out his plays first.

STONE. Remind me to sleep with a bazooka tonight.

PARLOR. Call everyone in one by one and we'll ask some questions. Nobody but you, me and Lady Riverdale know the chocolate is poison, right?

STONE. Edith and Ralph know but they won't blab.

PARLOR. Fine. We'll ask a few questions and offer them some chocolate. If they refuse, then we'll know they must be the killer.

STONE. What if they accept?

PARLOR. We won't let them have any. We don't want to kill them.

STONE. That's right. This is the second act. *(Leans to the intercom box)* I hate this thing. *(Pushes button)* Hello?

VOICE. Hey, good buddy, this is the Hurtlin' Turtle on CB Radio 215701264 KHZ. I'm going south on 95 watchin' for Smokeys. What's your handle, big daddy? Ten-four.

STONE. No handles, just door knobs. *(Looks at watch)* And it's 8:10. *(Punches button)* Powerful box. Hello?

VOICE. I'd like a pepperoni pizza to go, please.

STONE. *(Groans, punches button)* I feel like a radio talk show host. Hello?

DYSLEXIA'S VOICE. Hello? What can I do for you, Mr. Stone? *(PARLOR signals, to have her come in)*

STONE. Come in here, please.

DYSLEXIA. Should I bring a pad?

STONE. No, I have a cushion we can use. *(Punches button)* I don't—

FEMALE VOICE ON BOX. *(Very sexy-sounding)* Hi, my name is Veronica and I'm a Libra and I like skiing and mud-wrestling and would like to have a very meaningful relationship approximately 24 hours in length and—

STONE. *(Punches button)* I'll get back to that one later.

PARLOR. Now, it's very important that we be nonchalant and unassuming. We can't let them know that we're up to something. *(DYSLEXIA knocks and enters left)*

DYSLEXIA. Yes, sir?

STONE. Come in and sit down, please. *(She does. He grabs the box of chocolates and thrusts it at her)* Want a chocolate?

DYSLEXIA. Huh?

PARLOR. *(Giving Stone a nasty look)* We wanted to ask you a few questions.

DYSLEXIA. I'll help in whatever way I can.

PARLOR. Thank you, Dyslexia. That's an unusual name. Where did you get it?

DYSLEXIA. My father was a doctor specializing in functional disorders.

PARLOR. I see.

STONE. *(Abruptly)* Where were you on the night of December 17th of last year? What's the capital of Iowa? What did the Irishman say to the Isrealite? Did you kill Edith Chiles and Ralph Deadwood?

PARLOR. Stone!

DYSLEXIA. I was at home on December 17th. I think Des Moines is the capital of Iowa. I don't know what the Irishman said to the Isrealite and, no, I didn't kill Edith Chiles or Ralph Deadwood.

STONE. Good girl. *(Offers box)* Have a chocolate.

DYSLEXIA. No thank you.

STONE. Aha!

PARLOR. Stone, *please! (To Dyslexia)* Thank you, Dyslexia. Have Dick Simmering come in, will you?

DYSLEXIA. Yes, sir. *(She exits left)*

PARLOR. I said *nonchalant* and *unassuming!*

STONE. She didn't want the chocolate. She did it.

PARLOR. Not so fast. Let's see what happens with the others. Besides, *why* would Dyslexia do it? What's her motive?

STONE. This is the 20th century—you don't have to have a motive anymore.

PARLOR. You think she's a mad poisoner? She's so meek and cool.

STONE. It's a front to throw us off. And to think that I wanted to chase her around my desk.

PARLOR. Hold on before we come to any conclusions. Maybe she *did* do it. Maybe she wanted to kill you for your job and Edith and Ralph just happened to eat the chocolate first. We can't know until we talk to the others.

(DICK SIMMERING knocks at the door left and peeks in)

DICK. Yoohoo. Anybody home?

STONE. Come in. *(DICK enters fully)*

STONE. Sit down, Dick. How's the aerobics coming along?

DICK. Simply wonderful. I'm looking forward to trying them out tomorrow.

PARLOR. Dick, are you aware of the tragedies that have occured today ...

DICK. Aware! Are you kidding? Edith Chiles almost broke three of my ribs this morning. I broke a nail too.

PARLOR. Did you know Edith very well?

DICK. We chatted a couple of times.

PARLOR. About what?

DICK. Cooking, embroidery ... those sorts of things. She reminded me a lot of my mother. I tried to talk her into some aerobics but she said she didn't have time. A few of my exercises could have done wonders for her figure.

PARLOR. What about Ralph Deadwood?

DICK. Aerobics would have been good for his figure too.

PARLOR. I mean, did you like him?

DICK. Not particularly.

STONE. Oh, you didn't, eh? Have a chocolate.

PARLOR. What didn't you like about him?

DICK. He always seemed so viciously cruel. And I didn't care for the way he treated Lady Riverdale. He seemed to dominate her. His hairstyle wasn't much to speak of either.

PARLOR. Were Ralph and Lady Riverdale lovers?

DICK. I wouldn't know the answer to that question. At times I thought so and other times I thought that she detested him.

PARLOR. Thank you, Dick. Please keep all this to yourself. We're trying to get to the bottom of things and secrecy would work in our favor.

DICK. I understand. (Stands) Well, do stop by my aerobics class sometime. I could work up some great exercises for a man of your build.

PARLOR. Maybe I will. Ah ... would you care for a chocolate? Lady Riverdale's special box. (STONE starts to exit)

DICK. No thank you. I'm full from dinner. Celery always fills me up. (He exits left)

STONE. That's two who didn't want the chocolate. Maybe Dick and Dyslexia are in cahoots.

PARLOR. Maybe. They could be secret lovers. *(Suspiciously)* Like Ralph and Lady Riverdale. I'd like to take a look at some of Ralph's things just to see what I can find.

STONE. Probably just dirty underwear. Deadwood may be dead but I still consider him a prime suspect. I don't trust him no matter what condition he is in.

PARLOR. I take it you didn't like him. Did you know him before?

STONE. In another life. He was a snake that got reincarnated as a weasel. Who knows what he'll get reincarnated as next.

PARLOR. And what did *you* get reincarnated as?

STONE. A health resort manager. Little difference, actually. He worked on the Strip. He used to front for a girl—oh, what was her name? Babs or something like that. I never met her.

PARLOR. Did you hate Ralph?

STONE. *(Smiles, shakes finger at him knowingly)* I know what you're doing. Next you'll be offering me chocolates. Forget it, I know your routine.

PARLOR. Like I said: *everyone* is a suspect. *(ALFRED and SWEET PEA knock and enter)* One at a time, please.

ALFRED. Who are you?

PARLOR. Ed Parlor.

ALFRED. Are you a detective?

STONE. Relax, Alfred.

ALFRED. Sweet Pea and I are together.

STONE. Awww ... going steady?

ALFRED. I don't want her questioned alone in her condition.

PARLOR. Is she pregnant?

ALFRED. No!

PARLOR. *(Looks at her stomach then back at Alfred)* Sorry. Alfred, you were Henry Meadowbrook's protege. I would imagine you were his closest friend as well. How do you feel now that some time has elapsed since his suicide?

ALFRED. How would you expect me to feel?

PARLOR. Bitter? Angry? Possibly vengeful towards those who you might feel drove Henry Meadowbrook to his death?

ALFRED. If you're implying that I poisoned Edith Chiles and Ralph Deadwood out of revenge, then you're mistaken.

STONE. Then why *did* you poison them?

ALFRED. I didn't. And I resent the accusation. Haven't we had enough torture and grief from you people?

STONE. You're right, Alfred. I'm sorry. *(Offers box of chocolate)* Have a chocolate.

ALFRED. I'd rather not.

STONE. Why not?

ALFRED. I don't like chocolate. *(SWEET PEA mutters that she would like one)* She says she would like one. *(STONE and PARLOR exchange glances as STONE offers it to her. She takes it, slowly unwraps the foil, and starts to put it to her mouth)*

STONE. Wait! *(She stops and mumbles what is wrong)*

ALFRED. What's wrong?

STONE. I ... I can't stand it anymore—watching someone eat themselves to death. *(He snatches the chocolate out of her hand)* Like it or not, we're putting you on a diet tomorrow. *(She mutters protest)* No need to thank me. You may go. *(SWEET PEA continues to protest as they stand and ALFRED tries to lead her out)*

ALFRED. I don't know that her psychoanalyst will approve.

STONE. Why? Does he charge by the pound? *(They exit left)* That was close. She almost ate it.

PARLOR. Hmmmmm ... this is trickier than I thought. And that's good. It's just as I would have written it. Vague comments, shaded clues, a variety of suspects.

STONE. I'm glad you're enjoying this.

PARLOR. If Sweet Pea were the murderer, she may have known which chocolates were poisoned and knew which one to pick. She could have been calling our bluff just to throw us off.

STONE. Or Alfred.

PARLOR. Maybe. His could be a motive of revenge even though he denies it.

STONE. I don't know of too many killers who would readily admit their guilt.

PARLOR. This is wonderful.

STONE. You're crazy. Frankly, I don't want any of those people to come within ten feet of me without being strip-searched first. As far as I'm concerned, *everybody* did it. It's a group effort to oust me as manager and I'm willing to give in to their vote.

PARLOR. Don't get paranoid.

STONE. Paranoid! Have you all been talking about me being paranoid?

PARLOR. You can't give up now. I told you—we're safe.

STONE. I don't feel safe—second act or no

second act. *(ANNE enters left)*

ANNE. You wanted to see me?

PARLOR. Yes, we'd like to ask you some questions. You're Anne, right?

ANNE. *(Breaking down into tears)* I didn't do it. I swear I didn't do it! Honest. Cross my heart and hope to die, stick a needle in—

PARLOR. Relax, relax.

STONE. Take some valium if you've got 'em.

ANNE. Okay. *(She puts her hand into her pocket and pops a couple of pills)* Thanks.

PARLOR. Do you take those a lot?

ANNE. Only when I'm under a lot of stress.

PARLOR. And how often is that?

ANNE. Most of the time. Except when I'm asleep. My parents really wanted me to be a lawyer but I like medicine. I'd like to be a doctor except I don't like to hang around sick people. But I didn't kill those people, honest I didn't. I know you think I did because I have access to the poison and all but I really didn't do it.

PARLOR. Have you noticed anything even remotely poisonous missing from your supplies?

ANNE. No.

STONE. *(Offering her chocolate)* Would you like a chocolate?

ANNE. Sure! *(She reaches but withdraws)* No, I better not. They make me break out. I'd hate to be all pimply for the big day tomorrow.

PARLOR. We understand. Do you think that— *(He is interrupted by LADY RIVERDALE entering left. She is angry)*

LADY R. Will somebody please tell me what's going on here? Everyone's agitated that they're suspected of murdering Edith and Ralph. *(Looks at Anne)* What are you doing here?

ANNE. *(Breaking down, crying again)* I didn't do it! Honest, I didn't!

PARLOR. We're just asking a few questions to try and track down the killer.

ANNE. It isn't me!

LADY R. *(Annoyed)* Anne, please leave us alone. Go take a valium or something. *(She brightens up, reaches into her pocket and takes yet another couple of pills then exits left)* Gentlemen, let's understand something... I don't want you to track down the killer. I don't want anything done until after the Grand Re-Opening tomorrow. The staff has to be in top form and *not* upset by a bunch of insane accusations and insinuations. Mr. Stone, I thought we had an agreement.

STONE. Look, honey, your Grand Re-Opening isn't going to amount to a hill of beans if the guests arrive and the staff has been poisoned in the night. Forget the Grand Re-Opening!

LADY R. How dare you talk to me like that! "Honey" indeed! You have a lot of gall, Stone!

STONE. Who writes your stuff—*Mad Magazine?*

LADY R. I don't have to take that kind of talk from anybody!

STONE. Not even Ralph Deadwood?

LADY R. What do you mean by that question?

PARLOR. This is great! A conflict of authority ... the ethical question brought to light amidst anger and fury ... perfect for a play!

STONE AND LADY R. *(Together—to Parlor)* Oh, shut up.

STONE. *(To Lady R)* You must think I'm pretty stupid. I've been all day trying to figure out how a rich aristocratic woman like you got hooked up with someone like Ralph. It didn't make sense. A love affair? Nah. You two had something else going on.

PARLOR. Very good, Stone! Now you're thinking.

LADY R. I don't know what you're talking about.

STONE. Sure you do. Why else would you hire *him* to be your gym manager. Becasue you had no choice. He had something over on you. What was it? Something from your past?

LADY R. Pack your clothes. You're fired, Stone.

STONE. You were being blackmailed, weren't you?

LADY R. *(Turning away)* I have nothing more to say to you. Get out.

PARLOR. Blackmail. It all fits. This is good, Stone. Where are you getting all this?

STONE. I'm making it up as I go along.

LADY R. Ed, don't indulge him in this farce.

PARLOR. Lady Riverdale, this makes you a prime suspect. You can refuse to tell us anything but the police won't be so kind. You have the strongest motive of anyone to want to see Ralph dead. You can explain now or you can explain it to the police later. Which would you prefer?

STONE. And with the police come a lot of reporters. I know how you like publicity.

PARLOR. Tell us what you can and we might be able to help keep it quiet.

LADY R. All right, all right. But I hate you for this. Both of you. *(Her voice has lost its sophistication and is now the voice of a woman from the street)* But I'm tellin' ya just so you'll understand that I didn't kill anybody. Got it?

STONE. *(Surprised)* You mean we're right?

PARLOR. Of course we're right. It's too perfect to be wrong.

LADY R. I wanted Ralph dead. Make no mistake about that. I spent years being hounded by him. All the way from Bennie's on the Strip to—

STONE. Bennie's?

LADY R. Yeah. That's how I met Ralph. He was my—

STONE. You mean to tell me that you're ... you're Bennie Morgenstern?

LADY R. No! I was Bubbles Malone. Ralph called me—

STONE. Babs!

LADY R. You know? But how?

STONE. I knew Ralph when he was on the Strip. I heard about you but I never saw you.

LADY R. Yeah? Small world, huh? But anyway. I didn't poison Ralph. I wanted to shoot him but he died first. And as far as I know there ain't no law against wanting to kill someone who's already dead.

PARLOR. I don't suppose so.

LADY R. And I ain't clever enough to put poison into chocolates. Or that clumsy either. I liked Edith Chiles.

PARLOR. Then who killed them? And why?

LADY R. I don't know. *(Her voice returns to the way it was, sophisticated)* I really don't know. *(Stands and fans herself)* Oh, my blood pressure. Gentlemen, I am at your mercy with what I just told you. I could be ruined if anyone found out about my past.

PARLOR. Your past? What about your past? *(Looks to Stone innocently)* What's she talking about?

STONE. *(Shrugs)* Beats me.

LADY R. *(Nods appreciatively)* Goodnight. *(She exits left)*

STONE. *(Pausing, after watching her leave)* I wonder if Ralph had pictures.

PARLOR. We don't have time for that, Stone. All our concentration must be on the case!

STONE. *(Frowns)* The case. But we know little more now than we did when we started.

PARLOR. Au contraire, Watson. It's all elementary.

STONE. You can say that again.

PARLOR. It's time for the bookshelf scene. *(Lights start to fade)*

STONE. The bookshelf scene?

PARLOR. Sit down. There's something about this room you should know ... *(They sit and the lights now fade to blackout)*

Scene Two

Night. The office is dimly lit and as the lights come up we see STONE at the desk. Methodically and purposefully he rises and moves to the bookcase. He pulls the side of it and it opens like a door. He disappears from view behind it. Suddenly, he peeks around-front.

STONE. The plot thickens. *(He rolls his eyes in Groucho-esque fashion and disappears again. The case slowly slides back to it's original position. The room is still again until a PERSON dressed in black—complete with black mask—appears at the patio doors. The PERSON enters—unidentifiable—and sneaks to the desk where he/she looks around. The papers get shuffled, the drawers are searched, everything explored. Then the room. HE/SHE moves past the bookshelf, it slides open a little and STONE peeks out. Seeing the prowler, he comes out fully still unnoticed. Behind the prowler he stays, watching then following as the PROWLER turns and moves back to the desk. This is choreographed with great care to maximize the comedy of it. Finally, for lack of a better weapon, STONE looks down at his hand, forms it as a gun and sticks it in the prowler's back. The PROWLER freezes)* Don't move or I'll shoot.

MARGARET. With your finger?

STONE. Then I'll scratch you with a hangnail. Identify yourself.

MARGARET. *(Pulling mask off)* Margaret Daniels.

STONE. Miss Daniels! How dare you come sneaking around my office without giving me time to slip into something more comfortable first!

MARGARET. I'm not here for a date, Mr. Stone. I was looking for some information.

STONE. I'll bet you say that to all the guys.

MARGARET. *(Turns to face him)* Where did you come from? This room was empty when I came in.

STONE. It certainly wasn't *after* you came in. *(Over-dramatic passion)* Why don't you just admit it, Margaret— you can't stay away from me. You lay awake at night tortured by the need to see me— to hold me in your arms and touch me with your ink-stained hands.

MARGARET. You're crazy. *(She begins to back away)*

STONE. *(Taking a step towards her with every step she takes away)* I'm crazy! I'm nuts! You know how I am when you dress in black.

MARGARET. Get back, Stone, I know karate.

STONE. You're into that, are you? You devil.

MARGARET. Something's going on here and I want to find out what it is.

STONE. It's love, it's passion, excitement! *(He does a quick Mexican dance as if holding castanets)* A ha-cha-cha! Can't you feel it?

MARGARET. All I can feel is your hot breath in my face. It's like staring down a charging bull.

STONE. *(He stops, suddenly turns away, his voice forlorn)* Go ahead and insult me after I've given you the best years of your life. Take the house, take the kids, I don't care anymore. *(Overdramatically moves to couch—hand on forehead)* Oh, the heartbreak! Oh, the senseless betrayal! *(He throws himself onto the couch. MARGARET watches him with hands on her hips)*

MARGARET. Oh, the overacting! Are you finished?

STONE. No. I think I'm working up to a major dramatic award with this.

MARGARET. Don't bet on it. Look, Stone, something funny is going on and I want to know what it is. No more song and dance routines. I want the whole scoop.

STONE. And nothing but the scoop.

MARGARET. I was supposed to meet with Ralph Deadwood and I can't seem to find him. Edith Chiles is missing as well.

STONE. Do you think there's a connection? They're a

very unlikely couple.

MARGARET. Why don't you stop beating around the bush and tell me the truth for once?

STONE. And what will you do with the truth, Miss Daniels?

MARGARET. Don't be evasive.

STONE. Okay, I'll give you the truth. Edith and Ralph are dead. They ate some of Lady Riverdale's chocolate and it killed them.

MARGARET. You don't know when to quit, do you? Where are they really?

STONE. In their beds. It's one o'clock in the morning.

MARGARET. I knocked on their doors but they wouldn't answer.

STONE. I wouldn't either at one in the morning. Everyone's asleep *(Begins leading her to the door)* and it's time for all good little reporters to put their libel away and go to slumber-land. *(Opens door left)*

MARGARET. Stone ...

STONE. Just listen to the silence of the night. *(A very high-pitched scream pierces the air)*

STONE. Must be a nightingale.

MARGARET. That sounded like a woman's scream. *(They both dash off stage left to the sound of hurried footsteps, confused exclamations and instructions. With great effort, SWEET PEA is carried in by the strained SIMMERING and STONE. They take her to the couch. MARGARET follows)*

MARGARET. What happened?

STONE. Make that a triple hernia. *(They begin fanning her)*

DICK. Twice of this in one day is too much for me. I'll never be able to do my exercises in the morning.

MARGARET. Why did she scream? Such a shrill sound of terror! I've ... I've never heard a woman scream like that before.

DICK. That's because it was me. I was going to the kitchen for a late night Perrier and found her unconscious on the floor. I thought she was dead! *(ALFRED enters left in robe and slippers. EVERYONE else— who will arrive eventually— should also look fresh from bed. Panicked, ALFRED rushes to Sweet Pea's side)*

ALFRED. Sweet Pea! Sweet Pea! Are you all right? *(He takes her hand and pats it)* Sweet Pea! *(She rouses)* What happened?

STONE. She was found unconscious in the hall.

ALFRED. Sweet Pea, speak to me. *(SWEET PEA mutters something about wanting a candy bar)* She wants a candy bar. *(LADY RIVERDALE enters left)*

LADY R. What's going on? I heard a scream.

STONE. It was probably the same one we heard. *(ANNE enters)*

ANNE. Is everything all right? Do you need a nurse?

STONE. What are you going to do— pass out on us again? Look, everyone go back to bed. We're doing fine. We don't want to excite the girl. *(ED PARLOR and DYSLEXIA enter left)*

DYSLEXIA. What happened?

PARLOR. What's the problem? I heard— *(He pauses to look at Margaret Daniels dressed in black)* Oh, hello.

LADY R. Will someone tell me what's going on?

STONE. If everyone'll calm down, we'll all find out

together. Okay? Alfred, get the story from her and translate, will you? *(SWEET PEA mumbles that she found a mysterious box of chocolates in her room)*

ALFRED. She found a mysterious box of chocolates in her room.

LADY R. Oh no ...

MARGARET. So?

STONE. Chocolates aren't good for you. Didn't your parents ever teach you?

PARLOR. Go on, Sweet Pea. What happened? *(SWEET PEA mumbles that she was going to bring the box of chocolates to Mr. Stone but someone knocked her out and took the chocolates)*

ALFRED. She was bringing them to Mr. Stone when someone knocked her out and took them.

MARGARET. Took her chocolates? I never thought they were that good. *(To Lady Riverdale)* No offense.

LADY R. Margaret, I think you should leave. This is very private company business.

MARGARET. But I want to know what's going on here.

LADY R. Someone please see Miss Daniels to her room.

DYSLEXIA. Come with me, Miss Daniels.

MARGARET. I refuse! This is a cover-up! I resent the treatment I've been receiving here. You're infringing on my Constitutional rights!

LADY R. We'll be sure to call the ACLU for you.

MARGARET. This is outrageous! It's illegal!

STONE. Any more illegal than breaking and entering? *(MARGARET stares at him for a moment—speechless. She turns and storms out left. DYSLEXIA follows)*

PARLOR. Why the black outfit?

STONE. She came to see me. But it didn't turn out as I'd hoped.

PARLOR. No clues?

STONE. Clues! Who was after clues?

LADY R. This is getting out of hand. Everyone is tired and tense ...

DICK. I'm past tense!

STONE. Grammatically I don't think that's possible.

LADY R. What we all need is a good night's rest. We must be refreshed for tomorrow.

ANNE. Rest! How can we rest with a murderer on the loose? I'd be hysterical if I weren't so heavily sedated.

DICK. Mysterious Chocolates ... people getting poisoned ... Sweet Pea getting knocked out ... *(Indignant) What's going on here?* I think it's time that we be open and honest with one another, don't you? We're all intelligent, civilized people who are able to communicate with each other. Right? Let's have a meaningful exchange and share what the problem is. Okay? *(Coaxing everyone)* Come on, gang, what do you say? Isn't anyone willing to do that? I'm even willing to go first. Okay? I'm up for being honest. We can sort our problems out and—

STONE. Dick ...

DICK. I can tell you what's on my heart. I'm not afraid. We're mature.

STONE. Dick, this isn't group therapy. We're not talking about divorce, infidelity and sex problems. This is murder.

PARLOR. *(Trying to take control again)* Sweet Pea, you were smart to try and bring those chocolates to Mr. Stone. And apparently the murderer thought you were smart which is why he or she knocked you out to take them back. *(SWEET PEA mumbles that her parents taught her never to eat candy unless she knew where it was from)*

ALFRED. She said that her parents taught her never to eat candy unless she knew where it came from.

PARLOR. That was wise teaching in this case because we believe that it was the cocolate that killed Edith and Ralph. Someone put poison in the box given to Mr. Stone. *(EVERYONE—but STONE and LADY RIVERDALE — react to this with alarm)*

DICK. The chocolate! I have a box in my room!

DYSLEXIA. I have some on my desk! I could have eaten it!

ALFRED. Why didn't you tell us before? One of us could have died!

PARLOR. To try to trick the killer. That's why I asked all of you questions earlier ...

ALFRED. And why Mr. Stone kept offering us chocolates. You two amateur sleuths could have killed us all!

PARLOR. I don't believe that or I wouldn't have done it. I know about these things ...

ALFRED. *What* do you know? You know of *fiction* and actors and actresses parading around pretending to murder and be murdered. You are *not* qualified to handle real murders and real killers!

STONE. Boy, I guess he told you.

ALFRED. I insist that we call the police immediately.

LADY R. No! I won't have the police in on this until

after the Grand Re-Opening.

ALFRED. Lady Riverdale!

LADY R. You *must* understand! All of our futures are at stake! If the Grand Re-Opening fails tomorrow we could all be finished!

ALFRED. And if the murderer *suceeds* tonight we'll all be finished!

PARLOR. Wait! Wait! There is more you don't know. We've made an important discovery that could put this whole case to rest.

LADY R. What?

PARLOR. We're this *(Holds up hand—thumb and forefinger slightly separated)* close. Right, Stone?

STONE. Huh? Oh, yeah. Sure. Does anybody want a chocolate?

PARLOR. Not *that!* I mean ... *(Gestures to bookshelf)*

STONE. *(Realizing)* Oh! *(Speaks confidently)* Well, ladies and gentlemen, as Mr. Parlor said, we've made a very important discovery this evening. *(He goes to bookshelf and opens it)* Henry Meadowbrook had a secret room! *(EVERYONE gasps, wide-eyed)*

LADY R. A secret room! Alfred, did you know about this?

ALFRED. No, ma'am. Sweet Pea? *(SWEET PEA shakes her head no)*

LADY R. What kind of room is it?

STONE. A reading room.

ANNE. *(Interested)* It's a bathroom?

STONE. Yes! It was his private one. And amidst a bunch of magazines we found ... *(He disappears behind the door and emerges with a small black book)* ...this!

DYSLEXIA. He had his toilet paper *bound?*

STONE. No! It's a secret diary!

PARLOR. *(Stepping to Stone)* A diary! Stone, you didn't tell me you found a diary. I only knew about the room. *(Proudly)* Found it myself. I may say.

STONE. I found it after you went to bed. It has entries up to the day that Henry Meadowbrook died. I'm convinced that it may yield some very incriminating information. *(More exclamations of interest)*

PARLOR. You mean you haven't read it?

STONE. No. I only *glanced* at it. But Meadowbrook seemed to fear for his life. He seemed to think that someone might be trying to kill him. Possibly even *poison* him. There may be a connection somewhere. As soon as all of you go back to bed—which should be right now—I'll read it thoroughly to see what else it says.

ALFRED. But Mr. Meadowbrook committed suicide. He was a very sick and paranoid man. Whatever that diary has to say, I doubt that it has anything to do with someone poisoning Edith and Ralph. Or any of us.

STONE. Maybe. Maybe not. There's only one way to find out.

ALFRED. Mr. Stone, on behalf of Sweet Pea, I think she should have that diary. I'm sure it's very personal and as his daughter, she owns it.

STONE. Under normal circumstances I would say that was true. But these are not normal circumstances. We have a killer to catch and this diary could help us.

ALFRED. But ...

STONE. But *what,* Alfred? Afraid of something?

ALFRED. Of course not. And I resent the implication.

STONE. I haven't implied anything ... yet.

PARLOR. I think I should go over it with you.

STONE. No. If it does contain a lot of personal thoughts, the less who see it the better. Now, all of you go to bed. Pleasant dreams, don't let the bed bugs bite. *(He begins corralling them towards door left)*

LADY R. I hope you know what you're doing.

STONE. Not at all. But I'm doing it well, aren't I? *(THEY exit. PARLOR lingers)*

PARLOR. Not bad.

STONE. *(Relaxing)* I played "Romeo and Juliet" in high school. I did both parts. It was a psychology class project.

PARLOR. The bait is out. Let's see if anyone nibbles.

STONE. Well, if they do they've lost my respect as a clever killer. I think this whole plan is silly.

PARLOR. *You* know that and *I* know that — but do *they?* *(Moves to exit left)* And ... be careful, Stone.

STONE. Are you kidding? You said no one gets hurt in the second act.

PARLOR. Not usually. Goodnight. *(Exits)*

STONE. *(Begins to follow)* What do you mean "Not usually"? Parlor! *(Stops, looks around suspiciously, then looks at book. Cautiously he goes to the couch and lays down. He props the book up on his chest to read it. The lights fade. Blackout)*

Scene Three

Much later that night. The lights — curtain — will come up on the

*office. This time it's lit only enough to identify a form on the couch
with a book over the head — as if having fallen asleep while reading. Again, a figure appears at the patio doors right. The doors open
silently and the PROWLER sneaks over to the couch. As a stark
silouhette we see the PROWLER raise some sort of heavy object
and bring it down violently onto the form. Once, twice, a third time,
and then the PROWLER grabs the book and heads for the patio
doors. Suddenly a light comes on at the desk and STONE is seen
standing behind it shaking his head disapprovingly. It should be
noted that the bookshelves are still open from the previous scene.
The prowler — ALFRED — stops and turns.*

STONE. Alfred, I'm so disappointed. I had hoped that
this time the butler *didn't* do it. But I guess that would be
too original.

ALFRED. *(Bewildered and confused, looks at couch)* I suppose those are pillows.

STONE. Yep.

ALFRED. *(Looks at the book)* And this?

STONE. "Winnie-The Pooh." A personal favorite of
mine. *(Holds up diary)* Is this what you wanted?

ALFRED. Yes. I suppose you wouldn't hand it over if I
asked you nicely.

STONE. Too late.

ALFRED. Then I won't ask. *(Pulls out gun)* Hand it
over.

STONE. The butler packs a gun. I thought that sort of
violence wasn't used in these drawing room mysteries.

ALFRED. Again you're wrong.

STONE. Why, Alfred?

ALFRED. Why what?

STONE. I think we're a little beyond being coy now, aren't we? I mean, I think I can understand why you killed Henry Meadowbrook. You *did* kill him, correct? It wasn't a suicide. You just made it look like one. But *why?* Wait, let me guess. You were not his closest friend but his closest enemy, right? You were his slave for 20 years — abused by him, tortured, humiliated. And finally you couldn't take it anymore. You killed him in cold blood and then made it look like he did it himself. Is that how it happened? Come on, be a sport and tell me.

ALFRED. You're a terrible sleuth, Stone. *(Holds out hand)* Toss me the book.

STONE. Terrible! I thought that was pretty good stuff for a bluff. Right, Ed? *(PARLOR steps from behind the bookshelf with a larger gun than Alfred's)*

PARLOR. Check. I couldn't have written it better myself.

ALFRED. That doesn't say much for your writing.

PARLOR. But why did you have to kill Meadowbrook, Alfred? Why didn't you just leave?

ALFRED. That's your problem, Mr. Parlor, and from what I've read, it's the problem with your plays, too. You've been acting as if all the clues could be assembled and then built into a logical answer. But you should know better than anyone that there's always an angle that isn't revealed until the end. Well... *(He pulls out a second gun even larger than Parlor's)* ... this *isn't* the end. And there's so much you don't know, so much you'll *never* know. I didn't kill Henry Meadowbrook any more than I killed Edith Chiles or Ralph Deadwood. But unfortunately I'll have to kill you two. It'll be easy enough. Two guns, two bullets, it'll look like you killed each other. The police won't have a hard time believing that you two amateur detectives got confused and shot each other.

PARLOR. You forgot that *I* have a gun, too.

ALFRED. Borrowed from Lady Riverdale. I saw her give it to you.

PARLOR. *(Looks surprised)* Ah ... yes, it is.

ALFRED. Lady Riverdale doesn't have a gun. She only has a lighter that *looks* like a gun. She probably just wanted to humor you. You've been so reckless with your sleuthing about.

STONE. Uh oh. Got any other good ideas?

PARLOR. *(Stricken)* Whoops. *(He points the gun at the wall and fires. A little flame pops out of the top)* Oh well ... I better be careful with that when I write the play. But you have to indulge me one last question.

ALFRED. I probably won't but ask anyway.

PARLOR. If you didn't do any of the killing, who did? *(SWEET PEA steps through the door left with a gun larger than anybody's)*

SWEET PEA. *I* did.

ALFRED. Sweet Pea!

STONE. You mean she can talk?

SWEET PEA. Of course I can talk. All that eating was just a cover.

STONE. Pretty large cover.

ALFRED. Sweet Pea, get out of here!

SWEET PEA. *(Closes door behind her)* No, father, I can't let you take the rap for me anymore.

PARLOR. Father!

STONE. He's a priest?

PARLOR. No! Alfred is Sweet Pea's father. I should have guessed.

STONE. Of course! Alfred is really Henry Meadow-brook!

PARLOR. No, you dummy, Alfred is Alfred and Sweet Pea is his illegitimate daughter. He was having an affair with Mrs. Meadowbrook!

ALFRED. It wasn't just an affair. We loved each other!

STONE. The butler not only did it, he did it with the victim's wife.

SWEET PEA. Henry Meadowbrook was an obnoxious tyrant who dominated everyone in his life. We stayed and endured for his money only. But I couldn't take it anymore. He was obsessed with fat. When my mother went five pounds overweight he nagged her to an early grave. I hated him for the way he treated my father and the way he ridiculed *me. Fat* jokes day in and day out. "Hey, Sweet Pea, maybe we should call you 'Sweet Watermelon.' " "Hey, Sweet Pea, maybe you should apply for group insurance." It was maddening! So I killed him. My father didn't know about it until he heard the shot and came running in. He was the one who made it look like a suicide.

ALFRED. I had to. I couldn't bear the thought of them taking her away.

SWEET PEA. But it wasn't just Henry Meadowbrook. It was *everybody.* You can't know pain and loneliness until you have to grow up *fat.* All the kids at school used to ask *me* for a piggy back ride. They tortured me as if being fat were the worst sin a person could commit. And now society is the same way. People hide behind pert smiles and say "Gee, isn't she pleasantly plump" or "Oh well, she has a nice personality" or all those other cute expressions for being *fat*. There are worse sins to commit than being fat, my friends. There's alienation, the horror of always being alone ... and murder! I put the poison in the chocolates to ruin the Grand Re-Opening of this resort. I didn't care who died, just so *no one* would want to ever come here. *(Laughs viciously)* It was so ironic to see you health fanatics *die* from *chocolate*. What a delicious scheme. I've enjoyed every minute of it. And I'll continue to enjoy watching the downfall of this resort as it's torn apart by scandal. But enough talk. Give us that diary. My father and I are going to take a vacation to South America and we don't want any records left behind.

STONE. Well ... ah ... I hate to be the one to break it to you but ... *(Opens diary and holds it up — the pages are blank)* There never was a diary.

PARLOR. It was a bluff to get the killer to expose himself.

STONE. Poor choice of words.

PARLOR. Reveal himself. Or herself, as the case may be. It was a great plan.

STONE. Sure was. It worked too. *(To Parlor)* Tell me, how does a playwright end a play when he gets killed before he can write it? *(MARGARET DANIELS enters through the patio doors right with the largest gun of all)*

MARGARET. Nobody move.

STONE. She's a pistol-packin' Mama ... Margaret, I think I love you.

MARGARET. I'm not Margaret. I'm Detective Judith

Marx from the State Police. I was sent here undercover to investigate Henry Meadowbrook's suicide. You two did a sloppy job.

STONE and PARLOR. *(Apologetically, not together)* Sorry ... we did the best we could... *(Etc.)*

MARGARET. Not you two. *These* two. *(Gestures to Sweet Pea and Alfred)*

SWEET PEA. What made you suspicious?

MARGARET. The fact that his hands were tied behind his back.

SWEET PEA. I knew I forgot something.

MARGARET. Now, drop your guns. *(ALFRED, SWEET PEA and PARLOR drop their guns)*

PARLOR. *(Shrugs to Margaret)* It wasn't real.

MARGARET. Smart thinking. *(Suddenly ALFRED turns on Margaret to get her gun. They struggle, arms outstretched holding the gun. It points to STONE and PARLOR — who panic and try to hide — and then to SWEET PEA who moves to help. The gun goes off. SWEET PEA clutches her side and falls to the floor)*

STONE. That should register on the Richter scale.

ALFRED. *(Giving up the fight and rushing to her side)* Sweet Pea! Oh, Sweet Pea! *(He struggles to lift her head up)* Speak to me, my darling!

SWEET PEA. I'm all right. It's just a flesh wound.

STONE. *(A beat)* Any response to that would add insult to injury.

MARGARET. *(Keeping gun on Alfred and Sweet Pea)* Call an ambulance. *(STONE does)*

ALFRED. Sweet Pea, my precious...

SWEET PEA. Father ... we almost made it, didn't we? Revenge had a sweet taste while it was on our tongues.

PARLOR. Wait a minute... that was good. I want to write that down. *(He scrambles for a piece of paper and can't find one)*

ALFRED. Yes, my love, we almost made it.

PARLOR. Hold it. Don't say another word until I find a piece of paper.

ALFRED. It could have been the perfect crime. *(PARLOR continues searching for a piece of paper and pen as noises can be heard outside of the door left. There is a knock)*

MARGARET. Parlor, take care of the door. Don't let anyone in.

PARLOR. But I don't want to miss this. *(Searches harder)* This is an office for crying out loud. You'd think there'd be a piece of— *(Pounding at door)*

MARGARET. Parlor!

PARLOR. *(Shouting at door)* Hold your horses, we're having a tender scene in here! *(Finds a piece of paper — starts to write)*

SWEET PEA. Thank you for all you've done, father. I don't deserve you or your sacrifices for me.

ALFRED. If I had to do it over again, I would.

SWEET PEA. I love you. *(She passes out)*

ALFRED. *(Weeping)* I love you, too. *(There is a somber pause)*

STONE. *(Hanging up phone)* Is she dead?

ALFRED. No ... just fainted.

PARLOR. Just fainted!? That's no way to end a scene. *(They all look to Parlor dryly. He shrugs as the lights fade to Blackout)*

EPILOGUE

The next day. Mid afternoon. STONE enters with two suitcases packed and ready to go. He sits them down, looks around, then goes to desk and picks up a couple of odds and ends. He picks up the notorious box of chocolates, grimaces, drops them on the desk again. LADY RIVERDALE enters.

LADY R. Ah, there you are! I would like you to— *(Notices suitcases)* What's this? What are you doing?

STONE. Leaving.

LADY R. Leaving? But you can't! It's our Grand Re-Opening — the guests have been arriving in carloads. It's better than I could ever have imagined.

STONE. Amazing how a couple of murders will draw the crowds.

LADY R. Yes... all that news coverage on TV this morning did wonders. I can't wait to see what happens when it hits the evening news and the newspapers in the morning. And to think that I was afraid of the publicity.

STONE. Silly you. Now that you know, you can make sure it happens a couple of times a season. Just to keep business booming.

LADY R. *(Giggling)* Get healthy or die trying. You said it, John.

STONE. I was a child.

LADY R. How can you leave me now?

STONE. I don't think I like the health business anymore. It's too dangerous.

LADY R. But I need you.

STONE. You'll survive. *(MARGARET DANIELS — or should it be Judith Marx? — enters left. She is jotting notes on a pad)*

MARGARET. I think I have all the statements I'll need for now. You know, I'll need confirmation from the lab but I found some arsenic in Sweet Pea's room and I'll wager it's what she used. *(Shakes head)* It's incredible what madness will do.

STONE. And love. *(He picks up box of chocolates and hands it to her)* I want to thank you for last night. It meant a lot to me.

MARGARET. For saving your life?

STONE. No. When I caught you prowling. *(He wiggles eyebrows)*

MARGARET. I'd like to forget that. Should I really eat these or take them in as evidence?

STONE. Evidence.

MARGARET. That's what I thought.

LADY R. Will all of the details of this case get out to the public, Detective?

MARGARET. It's hard to say. Almost everything comes out in the trial.

LADY R. Good. Very good. That'll help business.

STONE. What are you doing for dinner, *Detective?* My treat. *(Pause)* To make up for the chocolates.

MARGARET. Filing.

STONE. Can't you go to a manicurist?

MARGARET. You never let up, do you? I should haul you, Parlor and even you, Lady Riverdale, to jail for obstruction of justice. Do you realize how foolishly dangerous it was to hide those bodies and play investigators?

STONE. Everyone needs a hobby.

MARGARET. It's a *profession* to the police. Next time, call them.

STONE. *(Looks down at his feet and shuffles them like a chastized child)* Yes ma'am.

LADY R. There'll be no next time, my dear Detective. I'll close this resort down before I go through another night like last night. *(DYSLEXIA enters left)*

DYSLEXIA. Lady Riverdale? Could you come, please? We seem to be having trouble with some of the guests. They all want to stay in Sweet Pea's room.

LADY R. Yes, Dyslexia, I'll be right there. *(DYSLEXIA nods and exits)* Well, business goes on. I do *not* accept your resignation, Mr. Stone. We will talk more. *(Moves to exit)* Thank you for everything, Detective. Come back anytime. For you, our exercises are on the house.

STONE. It's too drafty up there.

MARGARET. Thank you. *(LADY RIVERDALE exits left)* So. You're leaving. What are you going to do?

STONE. Raise chickens. It seems appropriate after last night.

MARGARET. Stay in touch. Your testimony will be needed for the trial. *(Moves to exit left then turns and smiles at him slyly)* And you'll be taking me to dinner. *(She exits left)*

STONE. Yes, ma'am, Detective ma'am. *(There is the sound of a toilet flushing somewhere. STONE looks around, confused. The bookshelf opens and PARLOR steps out)*

PARLOR. It really *does* work. I might take a shower in

there, too. *(STONE moves to luggage)* You're really leaving?

STONE. That seems to be the question of the day. And the answer is yes.

PARLOR. That's a shame.

STONE. Why? You got everything you need from me. I thought I was the perfect idiot to help with your foolishness.

PARLOR. But it's not enough. I'm not sure how to *end* the play after the murderers are discovered.

STONE. This won't do?

PARLOR. I hope to come up with something better. Something more dramatic.

STONE. You writers are all alike. You have to over-dramatize everything you put your hands on. Real life isn't like that. I think it would be enough to have the hero pick up his suitcases *(He picks up his suitcases)* and just leave. *(He exits left)*

PARLOR. *(Watching him, thinking about it)* That's not bad. *(Suddenly frowns, deciding against it)* Nah, it would never work! Would it? *(Lights fade to Blackout)*

—The End—

SAMUEL FRENCH STAFF

Nate Collins
President

Ken Dingledine
Director of Operations,
Vice President

Bruce Lazarus
Executive Director,
General Counsel

Rita Maté
Director of Finance

ACCOUNTING

Lori Thimsen | Director of Licensing Compliance
Nehal Kumar | Senior Accounting Associate
Josephine Messina | Accounts Payable
Helena Mezzina | Royalty Administration
Joe Garner | Royalty Administration
Jessica Zheng | Accounts Receivable
Andy Lian | Accounts Receivable
Zoe Qiu | Accounts Receivable
Charlie Sou | Accounting Associate
Joann Mannello | Orders Administrator

BUSINESS AFFAIRS

Lysna Marzani | Director of Business Affairs
Kathryn McCumber | Business Administrator

CUSTOMER SERVICE AND LICENSING

Brad Lohrenz | Director of Licensing Development
Fred Schnitzer | Business Development Manager
Laura Lindson | Licensing Services Manager
Kim Rogers | Professional Licensing Associate
Matthew Akers | Amateur Licensing Associate
Ashley Byrne | Amateur Licensing Associate
Glenn Halcomb | Amateur Licensing Associate
Derek Hassler | Amateur Licensing Associate
Jennifer Carter | Amateur Licensing Associate
Kelly McCready | Amateur Licensing Associate
Annette Storckman | Amateur Licensing Associate
Chris Lonstrup | Outgoing Information Specialist

EDITORIAL AND PUBLICATIONS

Amy Rose Marsh | Literary Manager
Ben Coleman | Editorial Associate
Gene Sweeney | Graphic Designer
David Geer | Publications Supervisor
Charlyn Brea | Publications Associate
Tyler Mullen | Publications Associate

MARKETING

Abbie Van Nostrand | Director of Corporate
Communications
Ryan Pointer | Marketing Manager
Courtney Kochuba | Marketing Associate

OPERATIONS

Joe Ferreira | Product Development Manager
Casey McLain | Operations Supervisor
Danielle Heckman | Office Coordinator, Reception

SAMUEL FRENCH BOOKSHOP (LOS ANGELES)

Joyce Mehess | Bookstore Manager
Cory DeLair | Bookstore Buyer
Jennifer Palumbo | Customer Service Associate
Sonya Wallace | Bookstore Associate
Tim Coultas | Bookstore Associate
Monté Patterson | Bookstore Associate
Robin Hushbeck | Bookstore Associate
Alfred Contreras | Shipping & Receiving

LONDON OFFICE

Felicity Barks | Rights & Contracts Associate
Steve Blacker | Bookshop Associate
David Bray | Customer Services Associate
Zena Choi | Professional Licensing Associate
Robert Cooke | Assistant Buyer
Stephanie Dawson | Amateur Licensing Associate
Simon Ellison | Retail Sales Manager
Jason Felix | Royalty Administration
Susan Griffiths | Amateur Licensing Associate
Robert Hamilton | Amateur Licensing Associate
Lucy Hume | Publications Manager
Nasir Khan | Management Accountant
Simon Magniti | Royalty Administration
Louise Mappley | Amateur Licensing Associate
James Nicolau | Despatch Associate
Martin Phillips | Librarian
Zubayed Rahman | Despatch Associate
Steve Sanderson | Royalty Administration Supervisor
Douglas Schatz | Acting Executive Director
Roger Sheppard | I.T. Manager
Geoffrey Skinner | Company Accountant
Peter Smith | Amateur Licensing Associate
Garry Spratley | Customer Service Manager
David Webster | UK Operations Director

GET THE NAME OF YOUR CAST AND CREW IN PRINT WITH SPECIAL EDITIONS!

Special Editions are a unique, fun way to commemorate your production and RAISE MONEY.

The Samuel French Special Edition is a customized script personalized to *your* production. Your cast and crew list, photos from your production and special thanks will all appear in a Samuel French Acting Edition alongside the original text of the play.

These Special Editions are powerful fundraising tools that can be sold in your lobby or throughout your community in advance.

These books have autograph pages that make them perfect for year book memories, or gifts for relatives unable to attend the show. Family and friends will cherish this one of a kind souvenier.

Everyone will want a copy of these beautiful, personalized scripts!

ORDER YOUR COPIES TODAY!
E-MAIL SPECIALEDITIONS@SAMUELFRENCH.COM
OR CALL US AT 1-866-598-8449!